AN AMERICAN CONSCIENCE

An American Conscience

The Reinhold Niebuhr Story

Jeremy L. Sabella

WILLIAM B. EERDMANS PUBLISHING COMPANY
GRAND RAPIDS, MICHIGAN

Wm. B. Eerdmans Publishing Co.
2140 Oak Industrial Drive NE, Grand Rapids, Michigan 49505
www.eerdmans.com

ISBN 978-0-8028-7527-3

Library of Congress Cataloging-in-Publication Data

A catalog record for this book is available from the Library of Congress

Contents

Foreword

Reinhold Niebuhr was an American conscience in challenging times. During much of the twentieth century, he had firsthand experience of the economic transformations and international struggles that were reshaping the nation and the world. From a defeated Germany just after the First World War, to Henry Ford's Detroit and the Great Depression, through the Second World War and new understandings of global responsibility that emerged after 1945, Niebuhr was a witness to history who understood the significance of events ahead of his contemporaries. His judgments were not merely reactive. He made them with a long view of history and an understanding of human nature shaped by Christian theology. He had a place to stand that shaped his expectations and gave him something against which to measure events. That is still important today, when the secularization of our public life makes it hard to speak of pride and power in the theological terms that Niebuhr used, even though his analysis made as much sense to atheists as to Jews and Christians, and his circle of influence included politicians, religious leaders, and public figures from many different backgrounds. Claims of conscience now tend to polarize and divide us. Niebuhr's story is a reminder that conscience can also reveal what we have in common, alert us to our own limitations, and engage us in dialogue precisely on the points where we disagree.

Andrew Finstuen was among the first to see the ongoing relevance of this interaction between faith and history in the American conscience. His book *Original Sin and Everyday Protestants* showed how the very different theologies of Reinhold Niebuhr, Billy Graham, and Paul Tillich all probed the limits of postwar America's complacent materialism. His work as a historian and educator convinced him that Niebuhr's time has lessons for the twenty-first century, too. The question was how to explain Niebuhr's conscience to Americans who are understandably absorbed by the problems of their day and distanced from events six or seven decades in the past. Perhaps Niebuhr's way of thinking, which helped respond to the rise of industrial America in Detroit in the 1920s, is still relevant to the challenges of globalization. Perhaps anxieties about communism and the Cold War can tell us things about ourselves that we still need to hear.

To explore those possibilities for a contemporary presentation of Niebuhr's life and work, Finstuen initiated a lively traffic in emails and phone calls with scholarly colleagues in history and theology, who quickly agreed on the relevance of Niebuhr's story and the need for a new way to make people aware of it. That is how I became involved in the project, along with Jeremy Sabella, the author of this volume.

What made this effort distinctive among the many studies of Reinhold Niebuhr's life and work was Finstuen's contact with the distinguished documentary filmmaker Martin Doblmeier. His films, including *Taizé*, *Chaplains*, and *The Power of Forgiveness*, have often explored theological themes, and *Bonhoeffer* demonstrated his extraordinary ability to use visual images, personal reflections, and relevant texts to evoke the crisis of Nazism and the experiences that shaped Dietrich Bonhoeffer's response to it. Doblmeier saw at once the important connection between Niebuhr's times and his theology. He told Finstuen at the end of their first telephone conversation that "Niebuhr is America's conscience," and at that point they had the theme, the title, and the director, all at once. Doblmeier's subsequent development of *An American Conscience* taught all of us who thought we knew something about Reinhold Niebuhr how important and transformative the events of his time were, both for American life and for Niebuhr's theology.

With Doblmeier's creative energy and archival research skills engaged, Finstuen turned to Healan Gaston, historian, scholar of both H. Richard and Reinhold Niebuhr, and president of the Niebuhr Society. She provided a comprehensive knowledge of current Niebuhr scholarship and helped make contact with theologians, historians, and political scientists who could give us perspective on the full range of Niebuhr's activities and interests, as well as a sense for the personality he brought to his work. Stanley Hauerwas, Andrew Bacevich, Gary Dorrien, and Ronald Stone all became part of the project, along with Mark Massa, SJ, Susannah Heschel, Cornel West, and many others who contributed insights into Niebuhr's thought or recollections of his teaching and speaking. Special thanks is due to Elisabeth Sifton, who brought her critical editor's eye and her unique experience into our discussions of the film. Those who knew her as the editor of the Library of America volume *Reinhold Niebuhr: Major Works on Religion and Politics* were aware of her mastery of Niebuhr's thought. Those who knew her as Reinhold Niebuhr's daughter were not surprised by her ironic sense of humor.

As the filming got under way, Martin Doblmeier's creativity, technical skills, and attention to detail gave life to his script, which was a remarkable synthesis of the many voices he had listened to and a deft editing of just the right images, interviews, and texts into a presentation that effectively introduces Reinhold Niebuhr to those who have not heard of him and brings him to life for many others who have read and appreciated his writings. Jeremy Sabella played a vital role in these efforts. Having just completed his PhD at Boston College with a study of Reinhold Niebuhr's Christian realism during the Cold War era, he was available both as a scholarly consultant and an energetic production assistant who never flagged in his dedication to the project.

Since he had seen the interviews, talked through many of the ideas, and reviewed the archival sources, he was the logical choice to write this book to accompany the film and make it a resource for classrooms and discussion groups. His writing skills, clear thinking, and knowledge of Niebuhr's works produced something far more than a study guide. All of us who worked on the project knew that there had to be a resource that would engage people who had seen the film in a further exploration of Niebuhr's life and thought. Jeremy Sabella has done that in a book that is also a thoughtful introduction to Christian ethics, twentieth-century theology, and American religious life. This is a text that will take its own place in the literature of Niebuhr scholarship, and students, teachers, pastors, and scholars who may pick it up in relation to a viewing of the film will return to it again and again.

Both as film and book, *An American Conscience: The Reinhold Niebuhr Story* has a scope that reminds us of the resources needed to keep this part of our history alive in contemporary experience. Andrew Finstuen made this case to receptive audiences, beginning with Dr. Chris Coble, vice president for religion at the Lilly Endowment. Coble's encouragement was vital in the early stages of the project, and the Lilly Endowment's earlier support for Doblmeier's *Bonhoeffer* gave us all a sense for what might be possible with *An American Conscience*. The Lilly Endowment funded the project in the fall of 2015. The Arthur Vining Davis Foundations, led by Dr. Nancy Cable, understood our purpose and emphasized the importance of educational resources to ensure that the film would be widely used and discussed. They supported us in 2016 with a grant for final production, distribution, and continuing education resources. Special thanks are also due to the editorial staff at Wm. B. Eerdmans Publishing Company for their interest in Jeremy Sabella's manuscript and their efforts to speed it to publication so that it could be available along with the film.

When the Cold War ended and a new century began, many thought we had left the world of Reinhold Niebuhr behind. A couple of decades on, the shifting forces of globalization, long-standing religious conflicts, and resurgent nationalism and militarism are all reminders that change is the only constant in political affairs, and those who seek to articulate enduring moral and theological truths must constantly adjust their realism to new realities. *An American Conscience* traces those changes through six decades with the genius of Reinhold Niebuhr. He was not always right, and certainly not always ahead of his times, but through his dedication to the task and his clarity about human nature and destiny, he became the conscience of his generation. All of us who have worked to put his story into your hands hope that you will find him shaping your conscience, too.

ROBIN W. LOVIN

Acknowledgments

When Andrew Finstuen asked me to help him assemble a documentary on Reinhold Niebuhr, I confess to some initial skepticism; after all, we were academics, not filmmakers. But he convinced me that America needed Niebuhr's distinctive voice now as much as ever, and that a documentary would introduce Niebuhr to a broad audience. Two years later, that vision has become reality.

From the outset, we knew our project's success depended on securing a director with an established reputation in documentary filmmaking. Emmy Award–winning filmmaker Martin Doblmeier topped our list. When Andrew first reached out to Martin, we had little reason to think that such an accomplished documentarian would be interested. But he immediately saw the project's potential, and to our delighted shock, offered to produce and direct the film. Later on, Martin asked me to consider writing a companion volume to the film and generously granted me access to interview transcripts. In the months that followed, he included me in various aspects of the filmmaking process. Over the last year I have had the honor of observing a master of his craft at work. I am grateful for his unwavering encouragement throughout our collaboration. Thanks also to the Journey Films team: Nathan Dewild, Anthony Bellissimo, Joey Diaz, and Jen Quintana. Working alongside you has been a pleasure.

Early on we approached two highly regarded Niebuhr scholars to serve as consultants and advisers: Robin Lovin and Healan Gaston. When I first broached the subject with Robin, I couldn't help but think back to several years earlier, when he agreed to serve on my doctoral dissertation committee before he had even met me in person. He has extended that same graciousness in numerous ways throughout this project. His involvement has secured instant credibility in the eyes of prospective funders and participants, and his advocacy, expert perspective, and generosity with his time and resources have been critical to the project's success. As president of the Niebuhr Society and specialist in the Niebuhr brothers, Healan has drawn on her profound knowledge to improve virtually every aspect of this project, the present volume included. Sincere thanks to you both.

It was Andrew Finstuen who proposed the idea of a film, and he has worked tirelessly to keep the project moving forward. After countless phone calls, grant-writing sessions, meetings, and plane flights, his persistence has finally been rewarded. The film and book are a testament to his passion, resolve, and ability to inspire others with his vision.

Eerdmans editor David Bratt saw the merit in doing a companion volume to the film and provided invaluable support throughout the writing process. I am grateful to David for believing in the project, and to all the Eerdmans staff members who went the extra mile to prepare the manuscript for publication.

Various people deserve recognition for helping me produce on a compressed timeline. Matthew Newman's keen editorial eye and expert guidance throughout the revision process significantly improved the clarity and coherence of the finished product. The Sabella and Koenig families were constant in their support, and always understanding on the numerous occasions that I sought out a quiet space in which to write. My wife Sarah Koenig has been extraordinary through every facet of this project. She was patient when I disappeared into my office for entire evenings, listened intently as I talked through my ideas, and offered incisive input on each chapter. I could not have done it without you.

And finally, a special thanks to Elisabeth Sifton, Susannah Heschel, and all of our interviewees. It was a privilege to work with your reflections on Niebuhr's life, thought, and legacy.

JEREMY L. SABELLA
Kalamazoo, Michigan

An American Conscience

One might expect a Hollywood icon to grace the cover of *Time* magazine's twenty-fifth anniversary edition in 1948, or perhaps a politician or a decorated World War II veteran. Reinhold Niebuhr was none of these. He was an inner-city pastor-turned-ethics-professor.

Niebuhr was no typical cleric or academic. His analyses of the day's most pressing issues were at turns incisive, unsettling, and prescient. In response to early twentieth-century crusades for social change, Niebuhr highlighted the intractable character of race and class issues. While an isolationist America sought to avoid deepening European conflict in the 1930s, Niebuhr argued that the nation had a moral obligation to stop Hitler's expanding power. On the eve of World War II victory, Niebuhr foresaw the need for responsible American leadership in the postwar world order. And as the United States grew prosperous and even more powerful following the war, he reminded the nation of just how insidious power could be.

Time and again Niebuhr articulated the ethical stakes involved in social and political action. And he possessed the rhetorical genius to influence other great minds and movements: the civil disobedience of Martin Luther King Jr. and the activism of Saul Alinsky; the political realism of international relations theorist Hans Morgenthau and the thought of statesman George Kennan, who originated the Cold War–era policy of containment; the faith-based political outlook of President Jimmy Carter and the literary imagination of South African novelist Alan Paton. Nor was Niebuhr's influence restricted to the political realm: world-renowned evangelist Billy Graham once mused, "I need more Reinhold Niebuhrs in my life."[1] It is little wonder, then, that *Time* eulogized Niebuhr as "the greatest Protestant theologian born in America since Jonathan Edwards."[2]

The contentious political and spiritual environment of the post-9/11 era has renewed fascination with Niebuhr's capacity to command attention and respect from across the ideological spectrum. Drawing on an unprecedented collection of interviews with experts taken for the PBS documentary *An American Conscience: The Reinhold Niebuhr Story*, this book explores how Niebuhr continues to compel minds and stir consciences in the twenty-first century.

Karl Paul Reinhold Niebuhr was born on June 21, 1892, to a German immigrant family in Wright City, Missouri. His father, Gustav, himself a pastor, passed on to his son a love for both the life of faith and the life of the mind. Reinhold went on to obtain the degree of master of divinity from Yale Divinity School before accepting a call to Bethel Evangelical Church in Detroit, Michigan, in 1915. Over the next twelve and one-half years, Niebuhr saw his congregation grow rapidly, became acquainted with the complicated race politics of the city, and earned national attention for publicly objecting to Henry Ford's labor practices. In 1928 he accepted an ethics professorship at Union Theological Seminary, where he remained until his retirement in 1960.

Niebuhr has long been admired for his ability to exert influence through the written word. His analysis of group dynamics and social change in his first major work, *Moral Man and Immoral Society* (1932), informed strategies of civil disobedience in the civil rights era. His 1944 book *The Children of Light and the Children of Darkness* is regarded as one of the finest twentieth-century treatises on democratic theory. His early Cold War study, *The Irony of American History* (1952), continues to inform attempts to make sense of America's place in the world.

The depth of insight that was characteristic of his work grew out of an extraordinarily active public life devoted to the pressing issues of his day. He advocated on behalf of the African American and Catholic communities of Detroit in the 1920s; he helped launch an integrated farming cooperative in the Mississippi Delta in the 1930s; he consulted for the State Department in the 1940s; and he spent countless weekends

1. Mark Silk, *Spiritual Politics: Religion and America Since World War II* (New York: Simon and Schuster, 1988), 101.

2. "The Death of a Christian Realist," *Time*, June 14, 1971.

preaching at university chapels across the country. Although a series of strokes in 1952 significantly curtailed his activity, he continued to write extensively. In addition to his twenty-one books, it is estimated that he published over 2,600 articles in journals, magazines, and newspapers.[3]

But such relentless engagement inevitably exposes one's shortcomings. As incisive as Niebuhr's analyses of race dynamics were early in his career, he has been rightly criticized for urging restraint at the precise moments when the civil rights movement most required decisive action. Feminist critics have pointed out that Niebuhr's emphasis on pride as the prime manifestation of sin neglects how sexism can make it extremely difficult for women to cultivate self-respect. In other words, as beneficial as his strategies for subduing pride might be for the powerful, they are harmful to those whose sense of self is fragmented by unjust power dynamics.[4] Others have argued that Niebuhr's case for the responsible use of power helped perpetuate the same abusive behaviors he critiqued.

In a sense, these lapses in practical application are intimately connected with some of his core insights. Niebuhr reveled in the paradoxes that characterize human existence. He envisioned human beings as both finite and free, subject to the limits of time and space yet capable of imagining possibilities that transcend these limits. He saw the human will as both radically good and radically flawed, able to accomplish great things, yet vulnerable to the distortive power of sin that attends even the noblest human endeavors. Niebuhr's own life and work embody these paradoxes. In spite of this—or perhaps even because of it—Niebuhr continues to startle us out of complacency, spur us to trenchant self-critique, and inspire us with hope in our struggles against the disheartening issues of our day.

The chapters that follow draw on the transcripts of interviews conducted by acclaimed filmmaker Martin Doblmeier for the documentary *An American Conscience: The Reinhold Niebuhr Story*. The film's contributors are strikingly similar to the contemporaries that Niebuhr influenced: academics and activists, politicians and journalists from across the ideological spectrum and at the top of their respective fields. Some even knew Niebuhr personally and are thus able to convey a sense of Niebuhr the

---

3. Larry Rasmussen, ed., *Reinhold Niebuhr: Theologian of Public Life* (Minneapolis: Fortress, 1991), ix.

4. Judith Plaskow, *Sex, Sin, and Grace: Women's Experience and the Theologies of Reinhold Niebuhr and Paul Tillich* (Washington, DC: University Press of America, 1980).

professor, preacher, family man, and friend. On the whole, they paint an intricate portrait of Niebuhr's legacy and enduring relevance in a twenty-first-century context.

Chapter 1 looks at Niebuhr's career as a pastor in Detroit. Niebuhr once claimed that his Detroit pastorate "affected my development more than any books I might have read."[5] It is fitting, then, that an introduction to Niebuhr's life and thought would begin with a close look at this period. The chapter traces the growth of his congregation, the evolution of the city, and his confrontation with Henry Ford. It concludes with an analysis of Niebuhr's first major work, *Moral Man and Immoral Society* (1932), in which he synthesizes what he learned during his pastorate.

Chapter 2 examines Niebuhr's activities from the early 1930s up through the start of World War II. This extraordinarily fertile period in Niebuhr's development marks his rise to prominence. At home, he expanded his analysis of race and class issues; internationally, he became only the fifth American ever to deliver the prestigious Gifford Lectures in Scotland. This chapter also explores the particular ties to Europe that enabled Niebuhr to observe and assess the chaos enveloping the continent, and to make his highly influential case for American involvement in World War II.

Chapter 3 explores Niebuhr's role in the aftermath of World War II and during the early Cold War. As the Allied powers drew closer to victory, Niebuhr foresaw the need for a democratic theory that would foster the responsible exercise of American power in a radically altered postwar world. He maintained that the democratic system of checks and balances was uniquely effective at harnessing the human potential for good and restraining the human potential for evil. Yet past variants of democratic theory had proven too naïve in their assessments of evil to calibrate these checks and balances properly. Building a more stable world order required democracies to take seriously the deeply problematic aspects of human nature that the chaos of the early twentieth century had revealed so starkly. This line of thinking garnered Niebuhr admirers in both domestic and foreign policy circles, giving him considerable influence over American culture during this period.

Chapter 4 examines the early 1950s up through the civil rights move-

5. Reinhold Niebuhr, "Intellectual Autobiography," in *Reinhold Niebuhr: His Religious, Social, and Political Thought*, ed. Charles W. Kegley and Robert Bretall (New York: Macmillan, 1956), 5.

ments of the 1960s. Niebuhr grew concerned with the spiritual effects of the unprecedented power and material prosperity that the United States enjoyed at the start of the 1950s. Where others pointed to sky-rocketing church attendance and the ascent of evangelists such as Billy Graham to celebrity status as evidence of religious revival, Niebuhr saw a culture characterized by spiritual complacency and empty religiosity. Where others saw overwhelming American power as evidence of divine favor, Niebuhr saw a nation oblivious to power's corrosive effects on the human spirit. Contradicting the optimism of the era came at a price, as Niebuhr got shut out of the corridors of power that had welcomed him several years earlier. Niebuhr also disappointed major civil rights figures for urging moderation and neglecting to speak out at crucial moments in the civil rights struggle. In short, this era showcases both the visionary brilliance and the practical shortcomings of Niebuhr's approach.

The fifth and final chapter offers an assessment of Niebuhr's legacy. During his Detroit years, Niebuhr described effective pastoral ministry as requiring "the knowledge of a social scientist and the imagination of a poet, the executive talents of a business man and the mental discipline of a philosopher."[6] Over the course of his career, Niebuhr himself ana-lyzed cultural trends with the acuity of a social scientist; deployed turns of phrase with the panache of a poet; launched journals, political cam-paigns, and organizations with the savvy of a businessman; and analyzed contemporary issues with an intellectual incisiveness that even religion's "cultured despisers" came to admire. And he took to his tasks with a pro-phetic zeal that enabled him to function as a voice of conscience through the tumult and confusion of the twentieth century. As the contributors to these chapters attest, Niebuhr's words continue to resonate in our own unsettling times.

6. Reinhold Niebuhr, *Leaves from the Notebook of a Tamed Cynic* (Louisville: West-minster John Knox, 1980), 138.

CHAPTER ONE

The Preacher-Activist

O n a Sunday morning in August of 1915, a fresh-faced minister as-
cended to the pulpit at Bethel Evangelical Church in Detroit for the
first time. He felt the mismatch between his youth—he was just twen-
ty-three—and the weight of the task before him. "Many of the people insist," wrote Reinhold in the opening entry to his published diary, "that they
can't understand how a man so young as I could possibly be a preacher."

But the new pastor was not only concerned with how he was perceived; he also chafed at the trappings of the pastoral role. "I found it hard
the first few months to wear a pulpit gown," he noted. "I felt too much
like a priest in it, and I abhor priestliness." Yet he also learned to value the
platform his vestments afforded him: "It gives me the feeling that I am
speaking not altogether out of my own name and out of my own experience but by the authority of the experience of many Christian centuries."[1]

Reinhold was no stranger to this sort of ambivalence. He felt it two
years earlier, in the spring of 1913, when his father, the Reverend Gustav
Niebuhr, passed away suddenly. At twenty years of age, Reinhold stepped
in and served as interim minister. He also felt it when, a few months later,
he enrolled at Yale Divinity School. He reported feeling like a "mongrel
among thoroughbreds" as he struggled to fit in socially and master the
academic nuances of the English language.[2] Yet from his rough-hewn

---

1. Reinhold Niebuhr, "Leaves from the Notebook of a Tamed Cynic," in *Reinhold Niebuhr: Major Works on Religion and Politics*, ed. Elisabeth Sifton (New York: Library of America, 2015), 9.
2. Richard Wightman Fox, *Reinhold Niebuhr: A Biography* (Ithaca, NY: Cornell University Press, 1996), 28.

prose, a brilliance showed forth that set him apart from his classmates. He received a scholarship that allowed him to earn a master's degree the following year.

In the summer of 1914, the siren song of politics nearly lured Reinhold from his studies. Carl Vrooman, a family friend who worked as assistant secretary of agriculture under Woodrow Wilson, had offered him a salaried job as his assistant in Washington. This prospect appealed to Reinhold's native interest in politics, and also would have supplied financial resources with which he might support his widowed mother and younger siblings. He eventually declined the offer, but not without a good deal of soul-searching.[3] Upon earning his master's degree, Reinhold accepted a pastoral position at Bethel Evangelical Church in Detroit, which belonged to a German-language denomination known as the German Evangelical Synod. His mother, Lydia, moved into the parsonage, where she took over the church's administrative duties. This freed Reinhold to cultivate and pursue the political life he had originally set aside.

As Reinhold adjusted to his pastorate, there was little to predict what lay in store for his congregation, or the city of Detroit, or the pastor himself. By the time he left, thirteen years later, to accept a position on the faculty of Union Theological Seminary in New York City, Bethel had grown exponentially; the population of Detroit itself had nearly tripled in size; and Reinhold had established himself as one of the most incisive and provocative thinkers in American Christianity. In the intervening years, Niebuhr would support and then critique American involvement in the First World War, collaborate with the Catholic and black communities of Detroit to take on a resurgent Ku Klux Klan, and publicly confront Henry Ford for unjust labor practices.

It is during the Detroit years that Niebuhr cultivated the ability to manage the divergent interests, identities, and responsibilities that converged uneasily in his life: his German heritage and his American identity; the life of faith and the life of the mind; his youthful inexperience and the authority of the pastoral role; his passion for social justice and the quotidian responsibilities of running a church. In the process, Niebuhr exposed the illusory nature of the dichotomies that others took for granted: between church and world, faith and intellect, religion and politics, the vocation of the pastor and the life of the activist. This sheer

3. Fox, *Reinhold Niebuhr: A Biography*, 33-34.

breadth of social engagement enabled Niebuhr to speak to his context in uniquely insightful, compelling, and unsettling ways.

The triumphs and tribulations of Niebuhr's time in Detroit shaped the content and tone of his first major book, *Moral Man and Immoral Society* (1932). It lambasted both religious and secular variants of liberalism, polarized intellectual leaders, and catapulted Niebuhr to national prominence. As Niebuhr looked back on his legacy late in his career, he noted that his Detroit years "affected my development more than any books I might have read."[4] Thanks to Niebuhr's time in the Motor City, religion in American public life would never be the same.

Taking Dead Aim at Ford

Imagine, for a moment, life in rural America at the dawn of the twentieth century. Farmers still relied on draft power to plow their fields and on kerosene lamps to light their homes. At any sizable distance from the railroad network, one traveled more or less the same way that people had done for centuries: by horse and buggy. For all the innovation emerging in large urban centers, rural life followed the same basic contours that it had for the Puritans and the pioneers. In the eyes of the vast majority of Americans, the "horseless carriage" was a plaything for the wealthy that smacked of decadent impracticality.

Then in 1908 came Henry Ford's Model T. It was mechanically reliable, simple to operate and fix, and designed to navigate the rough countryside terrain. The vastly improved efficiency of Ford's assembly line enabled him to mass-produce the Model T at an affordable price. And thanks to tractor conversion kits, the Model T could be put to use as a powerful and versatile piece of farm equipment. From urban centers to small-town America, Ford's invention revolutionized American life. At the same time, Ford created a reputation as a benevolent employer, most famously through his creation of the then-impressive five-dollar-per-day wage. It is little wonder that the public held him in such high esteem: he had provided ordinary Americans with unprecedented mobility and convenience and had created thousands of good jobs in the Motor City.

4. Reinhold Niebuhr, "Intellectual Autobiography," in *Reinhold Niebuhr: His Religious, Social, and Political Thought*, ed. Charles W. Kegley and Robert Bretall (New York: Macmillan, 1956), 5.

Niebuhr, however, was less than impressed with the cult of Henry Ford. In a series of scathing articles published in the premier religious magazine of the day, the *Christian Century*, Niebuhr took dead aim at Ford, marveling that the public held him in such high esteem "even though the groans of his workers can be heard above the din of his machines."[5] In general, Niebuhr's arguments were met with a mixture of apathy and incredulity. Few people were willing to attack the man who provided so many Americans with cheap cars and high-wage jobs. Indeed, Niebuhr himself had benefited from Ford's success. The construction of a substantially larger building for his congregation relied in no small part on the generosity of parishioners who had become financially successful through their association with Ford. As Gary Dorrien, who holds the Reinhold Niebuhr Chair at Union Theological Seminary points out, Niebuhr was broadly perceived as criticizing the "goose that was laying the golden egg."[6]

Niebuhr was aware of these dynamics. Years of experience had taught him that even the mildest critique of Ford would be met with torrents of criticism. Yet he felt obligated to take Ford on. Ford's track record —his curious compound of idealism and cutthroat business practices; his presumption that his personal morality ensured the morality of his enterprises; and the way that he used his philanthropy to cultivate a reputation as a humanitarian, even as he squeezed his workers for ever greater profit —epitomized something essential about the American character. Thus, for Niebuhr, the *Christian Century* articles were not just a critique of Ford, they were a test of America's religious conscience.

In the late nineteenth and early twentieth centuries, a liberal Christian movement called the Social Gospel had transformed American Christianity. The Social Gospel called on Christians to establish the kingdom of God on earth by reforming oppressive economic systems. Social Gospel leaders took an optimistic view of human nature, focusing less on human fallibility than on the ability of good-hearted individuals to work for social justice. If Niebuhr could expose the problems with Fordism in a way that resonated with the general public, then perhaps the

5. Reinhold Niebuhr, "Ford's Five-Day Week Shrinks," in *Love and Justice: Selections from the Shorter Writings of Reinhold Niebuhr*, ed. D. B. Robertson (Philadelphia: Westminster, 1957), 108.

6. Journey Films interview with Gary Dorrien, April 6, 2016. Unless otherwise noted, subsequent quotes attributed to Dorrien are from this interview.

Social Gospel strategy of appealing to people's moral sensibilities could bring about broader social change. But if his efforts failed, then perhaps liberal Christianity fundamentally lacked the wherewithal to confront the unprecedented social challenges of a rapidly industrializing society.

Niebuhr's standoff with Ford helped generate the searing critique of liberalism in general and liberal Christianity in particular that Niebuhr developed in *Moral Man and Immoral Society*. Indeed, one could make the case that his career and legacy would have looked quite different had he not decided to take on arguably the most popular and influential figure of his day. How did this confrontation come about? The answer to this question has its roots in the early days of Niebuhr's ministry, when his adopted nation and his ancestral nation took opposite sides in the First World War.

A Crisis for German Americans

The prospect of US involvement in the First World War presented a crisis for the German immigrant community. On the one hand, supporting the American war effort became a way for German Americans to demonstrate their bona fides as good US citizens. On the other hand, fighting against the country of their ancestry felt like a betrayal. It is no surprise that a German American church would feel this tension very acutely—or that their pastor would feel compelled to address it.

In his first article to be circulated nationally, Niebuhr came out strongly in favor of the war effort. "The Failure of German-Americanism" was published in the *Atlantic* in July of 1916.[7] In the years following its publication, he would retract or revise nearly every position he took in this piece; however, the article showcased a passion for social justice and a capacity to critique his own communities that Niebuhr would exhibit throughout his career. In this respect, it foreshadowed what was to come.

In this article, Niebuhr argued that the German American strategy for addressing the so-called "problem of the 'hyphen'" was not working. Like every immigrant community, that of German Americans had to figure out how to navigate the tension between two divergent impulses: the need to assimilate to a new society and the need to remain connected

---

7. Reinhold Niebuhr, "The Failure of German-Americanism," *Atlantic* 118 (July 1916): 13–18. Quotations in the following three paragraphs come from this article.

to its cultural heritage. German Americans opted to absorb American culture while retaining robust German-language traditions, as was clear in their insistence on maintaining German-language churches. However well this balancing strategy might have worked initially, it was no longer feasible as the prospect of war with Germany loomed over American public life. The coming war would force the German American community to break with its hyphenated identity by choosing which identity would predominate and which would become subordinate. By supporting the American cause, Niebuhr moved decisively in favor of an American over a German identity.

On Niebuhr's reading, assimilation had proven difficult in part because of clashes between American and German value systems. German virtues were "individualistic rather than social," as manifested by wealthy immigrants who were "prone to attribute all poverty to indolence and to hold the individual completely responsible for his own welfare." This German paradigm contrasted with progressive trends in American society whereby the "obligations of the individual toward the welfare of his fellow man and society as a whole have been considerably widened, and the moral conscience of the whole nation has been made more sensitive."

The tension between these moral sensibilities came to a head as the American temperance movement reached its peak. Beginning in the early nineteenth century, temperance advocates had lobbied for the American government to limit or entirely prohibit the sale of alcohol, which they believed was at the root of social ills ranging from poverty to domestic violence. Prohibition, or the movement to make alcohol sale illegal, pitted American Christians against one another, as newer evangelical sects like Baptists and Methodists advocated complete abstinence from alcohol, while Catholics and older European Protestant groups urged moderation, not teetotaling. The contrast in Christian opinions was instructive for Niebuhr. In his *Atlantic* article, he argued that German Americans opposed Prohibition on individualistic grounds that on closer inspection functioned as a means of evading moral responsibilities toward society: "[German Americanism] claims to be fighting for 'personal liberty,' a principle that has, in the history of civilization, covered a multitude of sins in the mantle of respectability." In the name of preserving their personal right to imbibe, German Americans were prepared to oppose the sort of legislative action necessary to address the multitude of social ills that had alcohol consumption at their root.

The way that Niebuhr contrasted a German affinity for individualistic virtues with an American affinity for social virtues illustrates how immersed he had been in the Social Gospel. At the movement's theological core was the belief that the kingdom of God described in the Christian Bible had concrete social implications. By carrying out the gospel's precepts to care for those on the margins of society, and by fighting unjust structures and practices, Christians would fulfill their mandate to build the kingdom of God on earth.

The Social Gospel movement had far-reaching cultural impact: it energized liberal Protestantism, instilled and deepened social consciousness at various levels of American society, and helped catalyze some of the most important social reform efforts and organizations of the late nineteenth- and early twentieth-century Progressive Era, including women's suffrage and Prohibition, Alcoholics Anonymous, and the YMCA. Indeed, some scholars have described the Social Gospel movement as the Third Great Awakening, similar in scope and impact to the colonial-era religious revivals of the Great Awakening and the frontier-transforming religious revivals of the late eighteenth and early nineteenth centuries.

Niebuhr's complaint that German Americans emphasized individual morality and material success at the expense of recognizing their obligations outside of their immediate community was a classic Social Gospel refrain, inasmuch as it sought to persuade its audience to take social moral obligations seriously. He later came to the conclusion that the hyperindividualism for which he called out his own people was quintessentially an American trait. In retrospect, therefore, the scope of his argument had been too narrow: he accused his own ethnic enclave of a tendency that ran deep in American society more broadly. Although Niebuhr hadn't yet mastered the large-scale thinking that would come to characterize his later thought, in the *Atlantic* piece we observe him "learning to use this big picture of the history of Christian thought to help him interpret what's going on in the local community," as ethicist Robin Lovin puts it.[8]

The article also highlights Niebuhr's penchant for self-critique. His ability to operate as a voice of conscience was rooted in his career-long willingness to take his own communities to task, whether they were small-scale groups such as churches and civic organizations or large-

---

8. Journey Films interview with Robin Lovin, April 6, 2016. Unless otherwise noted, subsequent quotes attributed to Lovin are from this interview.

scale communities such as nations. Although his thought would undergo various major changes over the course of his career, this combination of Social Gospel drive to speak out against injustice and willingness to engage in relentless self-critique would remain at play in virtually every sermon, article, or book he would produce in the coming decades. As Dorrien puts it, "Social Gospel passion . . . is in him till the end of his days."

Postwar Disillusion

The United States joined the war against Germany in 1917. In the wake of that declaration, nativist suspicion of German Americans intensified, prompting the vast majority of German Americans to suppress clear displays of their German heritage lest they give the impression that they secretly supported the kaiser. Some, including Reinhold and his younger brother Helmut Richard, even felt compelled to contribute directly to the war effort. Sensing Reinhold's intellect, energy, and political acumen, leaders within the German Evangelical Synod appointed him the denomination's main spokesman in support of the war. Whenever pastoral duties at Bethel would permit, he went on speaking tours to congregations throughout the Midwest and helped to assemble literature for German American troops in training. Like many German Americans during the war, Reinhold wanted to show, beyond a shadow of a doubt, that his patriotic allegiances lay with the United States.

By the onset of the war, Helmut—more commonly known as H. Richard—had also become an ordained minister within the synod. Although quieter by disposition than his gregarious older brother, Helmut felt a similar obligation to support the US war effort. He enlisted and served as a military chaplain. No doubt inspired by his brother's example, Reinhold tried to extricate himself from his work with the Evangelical Synod so that he too could join the chaplaincy. His published diary, however, reveals profound ambivalence about combining ministry and military service: "What makes me angry is the way that I kowtow to the chaplains as I visit the various camps. Here are ministers of the gospel just as I am. Just as I they are also, for the moment, priests of the great god Mars."[9]

In his capacity as a supporter of the war effort, Reinhold sensed that

9. Sifton, *Reinhold Niebuhr: Major Works*, 17.

both he and the chaplains were divided in their loyalties. In biblical parlance, they were serving two masters: Jesus Christ and the god of war. This division of service was not sustainable. As the Gospel passage states, "No one can serve two masters; for a slave will either hate the one and love the other, or be devoted to the one and despise the other" (Matt. 6:24).[10] Yet, even as he recognized this tension, he could not help but feel inferior in the chaplains' presence: "As ministers of the Christian religion, I have no particular respect for them. Yet I am overcome by a terrible inferiority complex when I deal with them. Such is the power of the uniform. . . . It is the uniform and not the cross which impresses me and others. I am impressed even when I know that I ought not be."[11]

H. Richard also felt this tension, which he sought to resolve by enlisting as a private. "He believes that war is inevitable," Reinhold noted, "but he is not inclined to reconcile its necessities with the Christian ethic. . . . This is much more honest than what I'm doing."[12] The war ended before Reinhold could enlist in the chaplaincy or Helmut could find a way out of it.

As the brutal character of the war and its steep social cost came into focus, this conflicted sense morphed into all-out disgust. The elder Niebuhr spent ten weeks in the summer of 1923 touring Europe with a group of ministers, businessmen, and politicians on a trip funded by Sherwood Eddy, an independently wealthy graduate of Princeton Theological Seminary who served as secretary of the YMCA. The poverty of the French-occupied Ruhr Valley of Germany and the enmity between French soldiers and German citizens that he witnessed left a deep impression. As he noted in a diary entry, "The Ruhr cities are the closest thing to hell I have ever seen. I never knew you could see hatred with the naked eye, but in the Ruhr one is under the illusion that this is possible."[13] Having heard "horrible tales of atrocities, deportations, sex crimes, etc.," he noted wryly, "One would like to send every sentimental spellbinder of war days into the Ruhr." In light of his role as a sort of war apologist among the congregations in his synod, Niebuhr was consciously, if somewhat obliquely, taking aim at himself.

---

10. Unless otherwise indicated, all biblical quotations are from the New Revised Standard Version.

11. Sifton, *Reinhold Niebuhr: Major Works*, 17.

12. Sifton, *Reinhold Niebuhr: Major Works*, 18.

13. Sifton, *Reinhold Niebuhr: Major Works*, 18.

The visceral effect of his time in the Ruhr induced a dramatic shift in Niebuhr's thinking: "This is as good a time as any to make up my mind that I am done with this war business." He continued, "Of course, I wasn't really in the last war. Would that I had been! Every soldier, fighting for his country in simplicity of heart without asking many questions, was superior to those of us who served no better purpose than to increase or perpetuate the moral obfuscation of nations."[14] Strategic deception, in other words, is crucial to keeping a populace committed to a protracted war effort. And Niebuhr believed that he had engaged in that strategic deception, making him culpable for the war's atrocities in a way that ordinary soldiers, propelled and deceived by duty, patriotism, and blatant jingoism, were not. Whatever his intentions might have been, this hardly mattered now: "The times of man's ignorance God may wink at, but now he calls us all to repent. I am done with this [war] business. I hope I can make that resolution stick."[15] Niebuhr emerged from his visit to the Ruhr a committed pacifist. It would take the specter of another world war to change his mind.

Niebuhr's response to his European visit also marked a clear instance in which he used international politics as a lens through which to understand personal ethical obligation. Forty years later, in an essay honoring Niebuhr's contributions to political thought, the eminent political theorist Hans Morgenthau attributed Niebuhr's brilliance as a political diagnostician to his capacity to see human affairs *sub specie aeternitatis* —that is, from a big-picture perspective.[16]

We will explore multiple dimensions of Niebuhr's big-picture thinking over the course of this study. One dimension was his capacity to view the individual as part of a transnational community. From this perspective, each person is part of an intricate web of human relations. This web connects us to one another such that individual decisions can have global implications. Conditions on the other side of the globe can reflect the consequences of our actions back to us in ways that challenge how we think about individual moral responsibility. Niebuhr's turn toward pacifism following his experience in the Ruhr was the product of him

---

14. Sifton, *Reinhold Niebuhr: Major Works*, 38.

15. Sifton, *Reinhold Niebuhr: Major Works*, 38.

16. Hans Morgenthau, "Niebuhr's Political Thought," in *Reinhold Niebuhr: A Prophetic Voice in Our Time*, ed. Harold R. Landon (Greenwich, CT: Seabury Press, 1962), 109.

using a transnational perspective to reevaluate his ethical obligations. Though his assessment of these ethical obligations would change over time, Niebuhr's vision of an inextricably linked global community would continue to provide a vital grounding for his political and theological thought.

Activism in the Motor City

While the First World War remade European lives, loyalties, and boundaries, Niebuhr's home community was also undergoing a transformation. In the late 1910s and early 1920s, Niebuhr's congregation underwent explosive growth. When he had been appointed Bethel's minister in 1915, the church had twenty families; by 1920 the congregation numbered eight hundred. This growth was in part the product of Detroit's own rapid expansion as it emerged as the center of the automobile industry. Robin Lovin points out, "If we think of Silicon Valley as the center of American innovation and creativity and energy today, Detroit was that place" in the late 1910s and early 1920s. As droves of people moved to the city, various urban churches saw increases in their membership. But even in this environment, Bethel's growth stood out. Under Niebuhr's tutelage, it went from being an ethnic German enclave to drawing its members from a variety of ethnic and socioeconomic backgrounds. Bethel was notable for its appeal to young professionals such as schoolteachers, and it even drew several auto industry millionaires. Owing mainly to the largesse of wealthy benefactors, Bethel was able to finance the construction of a handsome and capacious sanctuary on a prominent avenue in Detroit. The new building opened its doors in 1921.

Bethel's exceptional growth was in no small part the result of the personal charisma and commanding presence of its minister from the pulpit. Perhaps more important than Niebuhr's ministerial style was the substance of his message. Lovin puts it this way: "If we ask why did Bethel church grow under his leadership, I think it has to be that people were hearing him preach and seeing in his pastoral leadership somebody that understood the real problems that were part of their daily experience and not just a set of ideals that could be preached in any community or from any pulpit."

In his sermons Niebuhr demonstrated in cogent terms how the challenge of the gospel informed the nitty-gritty realities of life in Detroit.

His success in crafting this message was due in part to the extent of his participation in his broader community. He was involved in youth groups and labor organizations, and became a highly sought-after speaker at their gatherings and conferences throughout the Midwest. This degree of involvement would have been impossible had it not been for two people: Reinhold's mother, Lydia, who took care of much of the day-to-day administrative work for the parish, and his brother H. Richard, who would make the trip in from Missouri or Illinois to preach on the weekends that Reinhold was away. Running the church was a family affair. Without Lydia and H. Richard, Reinhold would not have been able to immerse himself in the political and social issues that shaped his distinct, compelling voice.

Niebuhr's time in Detroit during the 1920s is primarily remembered for his engagement with race and class issues. As American religious historian Healan Gaston observes, Niebuhr grew increasingly concerned over the "disjuncture between the middle class culture that he was presiding over at Bethel and what was happening for workers as a result of industrialization."[17] Addressing these issues represented the culmination of a process of working out the implications of the Social Gospel in a variety of forums. Niebuhr's pacifism aligned nicely with the increasing number of Social Gospelers who came to view nonviolence as the only stance toward war that could be reconciled with the teachings of Jesus. Niebuhr also became a staunch advocate of Prohibition, a trademark Social Gospel cause.

If Niebuhr embodied the enthusiasm of the Social Gospel, he also exhibited what he would later regard as the movement's naïveté. In 1920 he became involved with the Interchurch World Movement, a St. Louis-based ecumenical organization funded by John D. Rockefeller Jr., of the Standard Oil family. Among the stated purposes of the organization was to put American capitalism on a surer moral foundation by improving labor conditions. The organization's reliance on the philanthropy of the wealthiest family in the world aroused a good deal of criticism. Although aware of this criticism, Niebuhr vouched for the sincerity of Rockefeller's Christian faith and maintained that this faith was reason enough to grant him the initial benefit of the doubt. The organization folded later that year, denying Niebuhr the opportunity to revise his initial observations.[18]

---

17. Journey Films interview with Healan Gaston, April 5, 2016. Unless otherwise noted, subsequent quotes attributed to Gaston are from this interview.

18. Fox, *Reinhold Niebuhr: A Biography*, 70.

Regardless, the tone of his assessment of Rockefeller stands in stark contrast to how Niebuhr sized up Henry Ford several years later. While Niebuhr did not question the sincerity of Ford's self-perception as a benevolent philanthropist, he no longer saw good intent as an adequate basis for withholding criticism. Sincerity, Niebuhr came to believe, could coexist with and even enable self-deception. But he arrived at this insight only after one of the most acrimonious elections in the history of Detroit catapulted him into the city's race and class politics.

The Ku Klux Klan's incursion into mayoral politics in 1925 brought Detroit's racial tensions to the fore. The growth of the automobile industry had prompted an influx of migrants from two of the most despised groups in early twentieth-century America: blacks and Catholics. The Klan resurged throughout the country during the late 1910s and early 1920s, and this resurgence was especially pronounced in Detroit, where membership skyrocketed from five thousand in 1921 to over twenty thousand in 1923. The invigorated Klan threw its political influence into the mayoral race of 1925, which pitted Catholic incumbent mayor John W. Smith against Klan-backed lawyer Charles Bowles.

Although an outspoken advocate of Prohibition, Niebuhr was so alarmed by the Klan's resurgence that he joined a select group of local Protestant ministers in backing Smith, the "wet" incumbent mayor who supported the repeal of Prohibition. In hindsight, this piece of political calculation might not seem particularly noteworthy. But at the time, this was a radical and pragmatic move: radical in how it put race politics in the spotlight, and pragmatic in its willingness to discard a key plank of progressive politics to support a "machine" politician. As a Catholic, Smith was viewed with suspicion by white nativist Protestants, who viewed Catholicism not only as unchristian but also as anti-American. Throughout American history, Protestants had questioned whether anyone who claimed allegiance to the pope could also be truly loyal to the US government, and they had depicted Catholics as unassimilated, and perhaps unassimilable, immigrants who clung to the worst habits of their European forebears. As a politician, Smith aroused criticism for his association with Detroit "machine" politics, the quid pro quo system that aroused the ire of Social Gospel reformers like Niebuhr.

Niebuhr's vocal and surprising stance garnered the attention of the local press. Both the *Detroit Times* and the *Detroit Press* ran excerpts from an anti-Klan sermon of Niebuhr's ahead of the election, which Smith went on to win by thirty thousand votes. Impressed by Niebuhr's talent, Smith appointed him chairman of the Interracial Committee, which was launching a study of living conditions for Detroit's black residents. Niebuhr worked closely with a diverse group of civic leaders, including several prominent figures within Detroit's black community and Fred M. Butzel, a secular Jewish lawyer whose unflagging commitment to social justice issues influenced Niebuhr's lifelong appreciation for Jewish social ethics. The data compiled over the course of the study convinced Niebuhr to advocate on behalf of the city's unskilled workers. Healan Gaston observes that Niebuhr began to "see in Henry Ford a perfect example of the kind of self-congratulatory welfare capitalism that he thinks is responsible for concealing the true dynamics of power." Ford had become a Motor City icon through labor practices that looked generous to the general public but ultimately fostered greater inequality and worker exploitation. If Niebuhr wanted to transform Detroit's economic and racial realities, he would have to start by stripping the veneer of benevolence from Ford's public image.

Taking on an Icon

In his attempts to draw national attention to Ford's labor practices, Niebuhr had access to a formidable platform in the *Christian Century*. With a national circulation of thirty-five thousand, it was the religious magazine of record.[19] Furthermore, as Niebuhr was a known commodity to both its editorial staff and its readership as the author of numerous unsigned editorials, he had no trouble convincing the *Century* to publish his pieces on Ford.

Over the course of his Ford articles, Niebuhr's logic for taking on Ford became clear. In Niebuhr's eyes, Ford wasn't simply another greedy industrialist; he was also an idealist who portrayed himself as a humanitarian invested in the nation's spiritual as well as its material well-being. Through this combination of cutthroat capitalism and idealism, Ford embodied the virtues and vices of the American psyche more broadly. In Niebuhr's words, "Henry Ford is America. If we judge men not so much by their achievements as by their hopes, not so much by what they are

---

19. Elesha J. Coffman, *The* Christian Century *and the Rise of the Protestant Mainline* (New York: Oxford University Press, 2013), 68.

as by what they want to be, Henry Ford reveals the true nature of the average American."[20]

Niebuhr's case against Ford rested on the treatment of his workers. Shortly after Niebuhr had arrived in Detroit in 1915, Ford garnered national attention by instituting the five-dollar workday. At the time, these were unprecedented wages for unskilled labor in a large-scale industry. Ford maintained that these wages would be enough for diligent workers to support themselves and their families without assistance from the city. A decade later, however, wages remained the same even though the cost of living had doubled. Furthermore, Ford had since instituted the five-day workweek. While he was content to let others think he had done this out of humanitarian concern, to give his workers adequate leisure time, the net effect was to cut one day's worth of wages out of every week and divert these funds into Ford's coffers. Not only did his workers have to contend with higher costs of living; they also had to accept lower real wages. Meanwhile, Ford continued to enjoy high praise for his generous wages and regard for his workers' leisure time even as his profit margins rose.

Perhaps the clearest example of Ford's hypocrisy involved a program for "delinquent" youth. Ford instituted a drive to hire sixteen to twenty year olds, ostensibly to "keep them out of mischief."[21] The Ford Corporation promoted this as a philanthropic move to reduce crime. Yet the net effect was to replace older workers no longer capable of keeping up with the frenetic assembly-line pace with strong, young bodies. Those muscled out of their jobs had no recourse but to seek help from the city. As Niebuhr observed, "unemployed Ford workers are the heaviest charge upon Detroit charities of any class of citizens."[22] He concluded, "Mr. Ford is celebrated throughout the nation as the most benevolent of employers, while human material is used with a ruthlessness and disregard for ultimate effects."[23]

As scathing as this assessment of Ford was, Niebuhr did not think that Ford acted out of deliberate malice. He noted, "It is difficult to determine whether Mr. Ford is simply a shrewd exploiter of a gullible public in his humanitarian pretensions, or whether he suffers from self-

---

20. Reinhold Niebuhr, "How Philanthropic Is Henry Ford?," in Robertson, *Love and Justice*, 98.

21. Niebuhr, "How Philanthropic Is Henry Ford?," 101.

22. Niebuhr, "How Philanthropic Is Henry Ford?," 104.

23. Niebuhr, "How Philanthropic Is Henry Ford?," 101.

deception. My own guess is that he is at least as naive as he is shrewd, that he does not think profoundly on the social implications of his industrial policies, and that in some of his avowed humanitarian motives he is actually self-deceived."[24] The cult of Ford would have been easier to demystify had Ford been more blatantly self-interested. His heartfelt ideals succeeded in masking his self-serving motives from the general public as well as from himself precisely because he combined sentimentality and shrewdness in a characteristically American way. To see through Ford's deception, members of the broader public would have to recognize the self-deceptive tendencies in themselves.

Setting Ford up as representative of broader ethical problems in American society raised the stakes of what Niebuhr was doing. These articles weren't simply an attempt to draw attention to a cause, or to advocate on behalf of a marginalized group; they were making a direct appeal to the social conscience of a nation. In so doing, Niebuhr was taking the presuppositions of the Social Gospel to their logical conclusion. Building the kingdom of God required convincing a critical mass of people to do the right thing. Yet Niebuhr realized that the vision of the "right thing" animating the Social Gospel movement had been too narrow. The movement had made considerable headway promoting social causes that could be couched squarely in terms of personal morality, such as Prohibition. However, building the kingdom of God on earth required more than individual moral rectitude; it also required reforming unjust social structures. The Social Gospel thus far had gotten little traction with issues that were structural in nature, such as labor and race relations.

In Henry Ford, Niebuhr saw a unique opportunity to apply the energies of the Social Gospel to labor- and race-focused structural reform. In addition to epitomizing the nation's virtues and vices, Ford happened to be one of the most famous public figures alive. If people could come to see the hypocrisy in Ford's claiming to care about justice while turning a blind eye to the abuses in his own factories, then perhaps they might confront and reform their own indifference toward structural injustice. But if not, what would that mean for the Social Gospel's—and by extension, Niebuhr's—vision of human morality? The Social Gospel presupposed that the rational and moral faculties of human beings were linked in such a way that appeals to people's reason would also awaken their consciences. Within this framework Niebuhr had every reason to think

24. Niebuhr, "How Philanthropic Is Henry Ford?," 102.

that a clear, rationally compelling series of exposés of Ford would prick the moral sensibilities of the thoughtful reader.

In due time, however, Niebuhr was left to confront the fact that his sharpest, most astute challenges to Henry Ford's reputation had failed. What vexed him most was not the impregnability of Henry Ford's image, or the fact that the business community of Detroit closed ranks against laborers and their advocates. It was the way that other ministers distanced themselves from social issues as soon as they encountered resistance. This distancing could not simply be attributed to a lack of moral courage. In a *Leaves* entry, Niebuhr noted wryly that a "minister I have suspected of cowardice for years because he never deviated a hair's breadth from the economic prejudices of his wealthy congregation" had recently gone on a "tirade against women who smoke cigarettes and lost almost a hundred of his fashionable parishioners."[25] These pastors simply did not see structural injustice as meriting the same sort of attention as personal vices. They seemed to presume that personal transformation was key to social transformation: get enough people to live in a morally upright way, and social transformation would follow. Yet Niebuhr's time on the Interracial Committee had taught him that personal morality was not enough. His polemic against Ford was premised on the idea that, even though Ford was exemplary from the standpoint of personal morality, he deployed structurally unjust business practices. But if not even fellow clergymen could be convinced to treat the structural injustices of their own city as meriting attention from the pulpit, then what hope was there for social transformation? The logic of the Social Gospel presumed that a clear-eyed and courageous group of Christians could use rational suasion and moral authority to awaken the nation's social conscience. But now a more basic question arose for Niebuhr: What if the Social Gospel lacked the tools to diagnose—let alone address—the nation's deepest moral problems?

From the Motor City to the Big Apple

Niebuhr would need some distance from Detroit before he could work through these questions in a coherent and thorough way. In 1928 he was invited to give a job talk at Union Theological Seminary, which at the time was the most prestigious academic religious institution in the country.

25. Sifton, *Reinhold Niebuhr: Major Works*, 69.

After thirteen years of ministry in Detroit, Niebuhr welcomed the prospect of a change in scenery, and made his way out to Union. Following his presentation, the faculty put to a vote whether to add Niebuhr to their number. His detractors, mostly from the ranks of the more eminent and established professors, were put off by Niebuhr's Midwestern informality, extemporaneous presentation style, and lack of formal academic training beyond his master's degree. As Americanist Mark Massa puts it: "Who is this little upstart, this little son of German immigrants from the Midwest who doesn't have a doctorate from an Ivy League institution?"[26] On the other hand, seminary president Henry Sloane Coffin perceived Niebuhr as someone who could bridge the gap between high-end academic inquiry and real-world concerns. Yet, even those who saw the value in hiring Niebuhr lacked Coffin's enthusiasm. Gary Dorrien notes, "everybody on the Union faculty could think of somebody else that they'd rather have." The faculty went on to approve Niebuhr's appointment by a single vote. In light of Niebuhr's subsequent influence, one cannot help but wonder how American life and thought would have developed had the deciding vote gone against him.

Niebuhr left Detroit amid an outpouring of appreciation. Although various sectors of the city were sad to see him go, they also took pride in the fact that an adopted son was taking a post at such a prestigious institution. Particularly telling were prominent voices in the black community that contacted Niebuhr upon hearing of his departure. John C. Dancy, the director of Detroit's Urban League, wrote, "Had this news come mentioning some other minister it would perhaps have occasioned no earthly syllable from me, but in your case that is something else again." He continued,

I do not speak for myself only, I feel that I am expressing the feelings and the sentiments of the great majority of Negroes in Detroit, when I say that there is genuine regret in the minds of the colored group of this city at your leave taking. There are many of us still mindful of your usefulness in trying to do those things which would mean for better understanding and better relationships between the races in the city of Detroit. To have you go without an expression of our appreciation of your services would be rank ingratitude.[27]

26. Journey Films interview with Mark Massa, May 31, 2016. Unless otherwise noted, subsequent quotes attributed to Massa are from this interview.
27. Reinhold Niebuhr Papers, Library of Congress.

In a similar vein, H. S. Dunbar, the YMCA's executive secretary, wrote, "to us in particular it seems almost a calamity that you should feel called upon to remove yourself from Detroit. . . . You know too well how respected and loved you are by members of my race."[28]

This is not to overlook Niebuhr's shortcomings on race-related issues. He was late in turning his attention to the plight of the black community in Detroit, and would come to regret that he did not raise the race issue more directly with his own congregation. As clear and vocal as he managed to be on certain aspects of racism over the course of his career, he remained blind to other dimensions of the issue, as will be addressed in greater detail later in this study. Yet the above letters highlight how rare it was for a liberal Protestant minister of a white congregation to advocate across racial lines in a way that regarded members of the black community as, in the words of Dorrien, "fully realized, equal human beings." This highlights an important trait of Niebuhr's: he was extraordinarily single-minded. It could be difficult to turn Niebuhr's attention to those issues, causes, and injustices that weren't already consuming him. But once an issue captured his interest, he addressed it with an extraordinary amount of energy, and showed courage in his willingness to risk his reputation defending unpopular positions.

In short order the Union faculty found itself with little choice but to embrace Niebuhr. He injected undeniable vibrancy into seminary life. Describing his "tremendous impact," Dorrien notes, "he's a galvanizing figure, students flocked to his courses." The Niebuhr effect quickly extended beyond the classroom. Biographer Richard Fox writes, "He instantly drew circles of students around him. They dogged his steps as he careened through the hallway, they sat wide-eyed in the common room after lunch and dinner while he issued rapid-fire commentary on world events. . . . They flocked to chapel to hear him roar and watch him gesticulate: his words flowed down like waters, his ideas like a never-ending stream."[29] Niebuhr captivated academic audiences outside of Union as well. In November of 1929, scarcely a year after his arrival at Union, Yale Divinity School offered Niebuhr an endowed chair in Christian ethics. By this point, even Niebuhr's former detractors at Union could not deny his immense and positive impact on seminary life. Henry Sloane Coffin moved to keep Niebuhr on the Union faculty,

28. Fox, *Reinhold Niebuhr: A Biography*, 106.
29. Fox, *Reinhold Niebuhr: A Biography*, 111.

offering him a permanent position that Niebuhr would occupy until his retirement in the 1960s.

Ursula

Among Niebuhr's legion of admirers was an Oxford graduate by the name of Ursula Keppel-Compton, who was studying at Union on a year-long fellowship. She was hardly the first intelligent, theologically serious, attractive woman to vie for Reinhold's attention. But once Reinhold admitted to liking "the way her mind works," it became clear that she had succeeded where others had failed. Perhaps it was her impatience with what biographer Richard Fox calls "ecclesiastical cant," or her quick wit and dry sense of humor. Bill Hudnut, the former US congressman and mayor of Indianapolis, recalls a story his mother, who was friends with Ursula, told him: "She and Ursula sat right next to each other at a lecture by this bright new theologian right down the street at Union Seminary named Reinhold Niebuhr, and after he was finished Ursula turned to my mother and said, 'grossly overrated!' in her clipped British accent."[30] This bit of dry humor highlights a key trait of Ursula's: as much as she admired Reinhold, she didn't place him on the same pedestal that others did. They regarded each other as equals despite differences of age, gender, and status. Reinhold and Ursula's daughter, the author and publisher Elisabeth Sifton, notes that they "appreciated the drama of this highly educated, pretty young Oxford woman capturing the heart of this, as he called himself, a 'yahoo from Missouri' — and they kind of played up the contrast just for the fun of it."[31] Although at twenty-four she was a good deal younger than the thirty-nine-year-old Reinhold, she had the more prestigious education and social background. This made her a clear match for an up-and-coming academic in the 1930s. As Robin Lovin observes, "Reinhold Niebuhr was joining a classic academic family pattern in choosing this brilliant and attractive younger woman as his life partner." Ursula also had the intellect and sense of self to match wits with him. She refused, for instance, to allow his mother Lydia to live with the

---

30. Journey Films interview with Bill Hudnut, April 12, 2016. Unless otherwise noted, subsequent quotes attributed to Hudnut are from this interview.

31. Journey Films interview with Elisabeth Sifton, April 7, 2016. Unless otherwise noted, subsequent quotes attributed to Sifton are from this interview.

newly married couple. And she helped make sure that their home life retained a sense of levity. Elisabeth recalls, "life was fun in the Niebuhr house and if he ever got pompous and boring my mother would never put up with that."

With her training in Greek and Latin, Ursula possessed a keen editorial eye. As her schedule permitted, she copyedited much of what Niebuhr wrote, and helped orient him as he engaged classic Christian authors such as Augustine. She would go on to teach classics at Barnard College, where she helped found the religious studies department. Back in the fall of 1930, though, it seems that Reinhold intuited what the subsequent decades would confirm: he had finally met his match.

H. Richard

In the fall of 1931 Reinhold's younger brother Helmut Richard Niebuhr took an ethics position at Yale Divinity School in New Haven, Connecticut, placing him a relatively short train ride away from New York City. Reinhold and H. Richard now occupied the academic posts they would maintain for the rest of their careers. Together, the Niebuhr brothers would transform the face of Christian social ethics in the coming decades.

Those familiar with the brothers talk of their contrasting personalities: Reinhold's helter-skelter bursts of eloquence and H. Richard's quiet, measured communication style. This contrast emerges in the way they wrote. Reinhold churned out editorials, articles, and books at an astonishing rate, publishing over two thousand throughout his career. H. Richard, by contrast, published a handful of books and articles. As Dorrien observes, "Writing is a kind of torture for him ... it's laborious and very, very careful." But the end product reflects the care put into the process. Dorrien notes that H. Richard's prose was "perfectly composed, and you can see the immense care that went into it." This resulted in "little books that are just perfect jewels." This meticulous craftsmanship earned H. Richard a reputation as a "theologian's theologian," and as the more sophisticated thinker and writer of the two. Sifton recalls that her father readily acknowledged as much: "he thought that Helmut was the finer thinker and clearer writer. 'True, I have the gift of gab, but Helmut is the better theologian'—that was family doctrine."

There were also crucial points of divergence between their theologies. This was partly the product of their distinct approaches. Mark Massa observes that H. Richard, who drew heavily from the emerging discipline of sociology, was "much more the academic, concerned with data and interpreting data." Reinhold, on the other hand, "was much more the ethicist, the Christian ethicist, concerned with using the texts of the tradition to make meaningful statements about the duties of believers in a complex society like the United States in the twentieth century." But their differences ran deeper than methodology. The one time they exchanged views on a political issue in a public forum occurred over the Japanese invasion of Manchuria in 1931. In a series of thought pieces, Reinhold defended the use of embargoes and boycotts against the Japanese, even though these actions increased the likelihood of war. Even pacifists, Reinhold thought, had to deploy tools of coercion that risked leading to violence. H. Richard responded with an article articulating a pacifist rationale for rejecting such measures. It was entitled "The Grace of Doing Nothing"—a posture that, scholar-activist Cornel West notes, "Reinhold could never entertain. . . . He's a dynamo. Every minute: change, change, engagement, engagement, transformation, transformation."[32] This highlights an important contrast in theological sensibility. Whereas Reinhold saw relentless human effort as key to transformation, West notes that H. Richard saw transformation as the "by-product of the quest for spiritual maturation"—a quest that requires punctuating the drive to constant, frenetic activity with stillness, surrender, and contemplation. Only then can you "connect the formation of your soul vertically with a power bigger than you."

Despite (or in many cases, because of) these differences, the brothers were able to balance, anchor, and exhort one another. H. Richard exercised tremendous behind-the-scenes influence on Reinhold's thought. It was H. Richard, for instance, who pushed Reinhold to reexamine the thought of Augustine, Luther, Calvin, and other thinkers in the Pauline theological tradition. Reinhold and H. Richard openly acknowledged the "differences in temperament" between them, even as they sparred fiercely but amicably with one another in their private correspondence and published writings.[33] There is no question that this intensive engage-

32. Journey Films interview with Cornel West, April 5, 2016. Unless otherwise noted, subsequent quotes attributed to West are from this interview.

33. K. Healan Gaston, "'A Bad Kind of Magic': The Niebuhr Brothers on 'Utilitarian Christianity' and the Defense of Democracy," *Harvard Theological Review*, no. 107, no. 1 (January 2014): 6.

ment spurred them both to greater excellence. Cornel West quips that "two of the towering theologians of the twentieth century . . . just happen to be from the same family." Given the considerable evidence of mutual influence, one has to wonder: Would either have achieved such eminence without the fraternity of the other?

Moral Man and Immoral Society

> Politics will, to the end of history, be the arena where conscience and power meet, where the ethical and coercive factors in human life will interpenetrate and work out their tentative and uneasy compromises.
>
> — *Moral Man and Immoral Society*

In the cosmopolitan setting of New York City, with Ursula by his side and H. Richard nearby, Reinhold had attained both the distance and the stability to revise his thinking in light of the Detroit experience. The result was his first (and arguably most influential) major scholarly work: *Moral Man and Immoral Society*.

Two key factors shaped the tone of the book. One was the market crash of 1929, which touched off what we know today as the Great Depression. Niebuhr's forays into New York politics — he joined the Socialist Party in 1930 and ran for the state senate as its candidate later that year — exposed him to the impact of the depression on both the city and the nation more broadly. The prosperity of the 1920s had provided enough of a basis for ignoring fundamental problems in American economic and societal life. As bread lines, gaunt complexions, and other telltale signs of abject poverty proliferated across the country, the signs became impossible to ignore. As Lovin notes, *Moral Man* was a book "addressed to a society in crisis. You couldn't write *Moral Man and Immoral Society* five years earlier. You certainly couldn't write it during the fifties."

The other factor shaping the tone of *Moral Man* involved the divisive race politics that emerged at Bethel after Niebuhr's departure. In January of 1930, the congregation moved to exclude blacks from church membership. Niebuhr was heartbroken. Rarely inclined to display raw emotion even in his personal letters, he described himself as "hurt and pained to my innermost being by your action," adding that "whether I shall ever preach in your pulpit again is a real question in my mind."[34] While not so naïve as to think that his congregants were free of prejudice, he was taken aback by the swift, blatant, and public way in which the church implemented racist membership policies after his departure. It must have seemed to Niebuhr that the socially conscious and inclusive ethos he had spent over a decade building at Bethel came crumbling down almost as soon as he had left. Could it be that he had built his ministry on a foundation of sand?

These factors combined to inform the tone and content of *Moral Man*. Within a few paragraphs it becomes clear that one is engaging with a consummate wordsmith. For over a decade, Niebuhr had churned out an unremitting stream of articles, op-eds, and think pieces. During that time, he had learned to turn a phrase with a provocative incisiveness that few can match, such as when he accused Henry Ford of applying the "social intelligence of a country village" to industrial problems, or when he quipped that "most men would like to follow Jesus and Napoleon at the same time."[35] Scholar Larry Rasmussen tellingly describes Niebuhr as a "dramatist of theological ideas in the public arena."[36] In *Moral Man* this flair for dramatic presentation of ideas is on full display.

A sense of righteous indignation pervades the book. The anger is contained yet sustained, a cold fury distilled into crisp prose. On the other side of mid-twentieth-century catastrophe, it is easy to see the book as prophetic and insightful, a bracing antidote to our own moral languor. But it hit Niebuhr's contemporaries like a thunderclap. *Moral Man* changed the face of theological discourse in America, and it remains, in Cornel West's words, "the most important text of Christian ethics to this day."

"Insofar as this treatise has a polemic interest," Niebuhr wrote in his introduction, "it is directed against the moralists, both religious and secular, who imagine that the egoism of individuals is being progressively checked by the development of rationality or the growth of a religiously inspired goodwill and that nothing but the continuance of this process is necessary to establish social harmony between all human societies and collectives."[37]

34. Fox, *Reinhold Niebuhr: A Biography*, 119.

35. Niebuhr, "How Philanthropic Is Henry Ford?," 98–102.

36. Larry Rasmussen, ed., *Reinhold Niebuhr: Theologian of American Public Life* (Minneapolis: Fortress, 1991), 1.

37. Reinhold Niebuhr, "Moral Man and Immoral Society," in Sifton, *Reinhold Niebuhr: Major Works*, 140.

As Niebuhr saw it, both religious and secular variants of liberalism presume that the trajectory of human civilization is one of continual progress: from ignorance to knowledge, from superstition to enlightenment, from brutishness to civilization. The engine driving the forward march of progress is the power of reason. Human beings, the thinking goes, are rational animals. The more they cultivate and apply the tools of reason, the better their societies will become. For Niebuhr this view was not only dangerously naïve; it was also based on a fatally flawed understanding of how reason operates in human relations. While at times the proverbial voice of reason can prevent a group from behaving rashly, people can also use powers of intellect to manipulate, cajole, and coerce others. The human will, in other words, can weaponize reason to do harm as well as good, and human relations attest to the fact that self-interest consistently prevails over generosity.

If Niebuhr's contention that reason is "always, to some degree, the servant of self-interest" is correct, then it is necessary to rethink the liberal understanding of human nature and human relations.[38] As his title suggests, Niebuhr conceded that individuals are capable of moral behavior toward those with whom they share bonds of affection, such as family members and close friends. The intimacy characterizing such relationships cultivates our altruistic impulses and suppresses our egoism. But once we move beyond our tight-knit social networks, the personal connections that activate altruism and contain egoism unravel swiftly. There are rare individuals who treat strangers with the same empathy and consideration that they do their close friends, but they are the shining exceptions. The vast majority of people behave morally toward those within their immediate networks, but self-interestedly toward those outside of their networks. As a result, egoism predominates in interactions between groups, no matter how moral certain individuals constituting these groups happen to be. Niebuhr's language on this point is unequivocal: to the careful observer, group dynamics always highlight "the brutal character of the behavior of all human collectives, and the power of self interest in all intergroup relations." This prompted Niebuhr to conclude, "the limitations of human imagination and easy subservience of reason to prejudice and passion, and the consequent persistence of irrational egoism, particularly in group behavior, make social conflict an inevitability in human history, probably till its end."[39]

---

38. Sifton, *Reinhold Niebuhr: Major Works*, 141.
39. Sifton, *Reinhold Niebuhr: Major Works*, 146.

Important implications follow from this. First, there is no clear trajectory of moral progress in human affairs: peace between groups is the result of a balance of power, not an increase in morality. Second, in order to advocate on behalf of a particular group, one must resort to coercion: there is no other way to obtain concessions from the powerful on behalf of the powerless. As Niebuhr states, "when collective power, whether in the form of imperialism or class domination, exploits weakness, it can never be dislodged unless power is raised against it."[40] By way of illustration, Niebuhr invoked the example of Gandhi, whose philosophy of nonviolence was pivotal in putting India on the path to independence from the British Empire. Niebuhr argued that Gandhi succeeded, not because of the morally compelling character of nonviolence, but because he managed to translate nonviolence into a form of political leverage.[41] Nonviolence was effective, in short, only insofar as it was coercive, and coercion was necessary no matter how lofty a given movement's moral vision.

In the realm of politics, the ethical question becomes not "How do I avoid coercion?" but rather, "How do I use coercion rightly?" Mark Massa puts it this way: "Coercion is a neutral thing. Coercion can be used for good, and coercion can be used for bad. . . . Because we are embodied creatures, it's just the way we get things done. If you tell a six-year-old . . . they have to stay in their seat and read when they want to get up and run, that is a form of coercion whether we like it or not." In light of the inevitable character of coercion, advocates of the Social Gospel needed to rethink fundamentally how the gospel applied to human affairs. The Social Gospel, according to Niebuhr's reading, presumed that implementing the ethical precepts of Jesus in society was a straightforward process. This presumption ignored, however, that while the ethics of Jesus are governed by the law of love, the political realm is governed by the law of power. Achieving justice in the political realm required using coercive measures that made it impossible for humans to manifest the law of love in an unsullied way. Social ethics required discerning how best to approximate the law of love in an arena that understands only power. Moral man had to be willing to engage immoral society on society's own power-driven terms. By failing to understand this, the Social Gospel had proved to be too heavenly minded to be of earthly good.

40. Sifton, *Reinhold Niebuhr: Major Works*, 140.
41. Sifton, *Reinhold Niebuhr: Major Works*, 322–33.

Niebuhr's argument was a stunning critique of liberal optimism, and by implication, the Social Gospel. One can sense Niebuhr working through various aspects of his Detroit experience: his inability to puncture Ford's philanthropic image through moral suasion; his sense of despair before the intractable race issues he encountered on the Interracial Committee; his regret over the way Bethel exerted its collective egoism to exclude blacks from its membership roles. These experiences contained lessons, not simply about powerful tycoons, the city of Detroit, or American society, but about human nature itself. Just as Ford appeared to deceive himself into thinking he was a paragon of virtue even as he exploited his workers, so we deceive ourselves into thinking we are basically good people, and thus justify turning a blind eye to group egoism. To begin effective work on behalf of justice, we must concede the inevitability of egoism in human collectives. This starting point generates quite a different take on the nature of social ethics than mainstream Christianity was espousing. Cornel West contrasts Niebuhr's vision for social ethics with that of his contemporaries as follows: "Liberal theologians were claiming that we were on the road to progress, that human beings were perfectible, that there was a possibility of some utopian society in history. It was a kind of captivity to a highly fashionable, secular claim about what the future could be. Niebuhr comes in with this tragic sensibility. . . . He says no, we all have fallen, we all are finite, we all are fallible. There will never be a utopian society in human history, there will never be paradise in space and time." Christian social ethics would spend the next few decades working out the implications of these contrasting visions.

In one important respect, Niebuhr remained a true Social Gospeler for the rest of his life: he fixated on how to bring about justice at the level of human collectives. But in the eyes of many of his readers, *Moral Man* struck a decisive blow to naïvely optimistic estimates of when and how this sort of justice would come about. Niebuhr injected a keen sense of the tragic into Christian social ethics, which subsequent thinkers would find difficult to ignore regardless of whether they agreed with him. The full extent of *Moral Man*'s impact would be felt twenty years after its publication, when a young graduate student by the name of Martin Luther King Jr. picked up a copy. As he went on to develop his notions of nonviolence and civil disobedience, King would cite Gandhi as an inspiration. However, it was Niebuhr's work in *Moral Man* that provided King with a framework for how to translate nonviolent movements into political leverage. Describing King's reaction to *Moral Man*, West states,

"My God. We've got something indigenous here. We've got something organic here. We've got an American intellectual who is acknowledging a degree to which certain kinds of spiritual gifts that black people have honed out over time can contribute to a struggle for justice by using non-violent strategies." Insofar as it shaped King's appreciation for the coercive potential of nonviolence, *Moral Man* helped lay the groundwork for key aspects of the civil rights movement.

Despite the wide-ranging influence and critical impact of *Moral Man*, it still had some key limitations. Critics have argued that Niebuhr emphasized the tragic dimension of the human experience without supplying a basis for hope. Regarding Niebuhr's assessment of human nature, King himself wondered, "within such a view, is there no hope for man?"[42] There are good reasons for raising this concern. *Moral Man* is a masterful work of social criticism, but it offers few resources for formulating a constructive alternative to the Social Gospel. Niebuhr would spend the rest of the 1930s mining Christian thought for the resources with which to revive hope in light of the tragic flaws he had identified in human nature and society. But even during this period of theological immersion, Niebuhr remained relentlessly engaged in the politics of his day, particularly as the specter of another world war loomed.

42. Martin Luther King Jr., "The Theology of Reinhold Niebuhr," Martin Luther King, Jr. Research and Education Institute, Stanford University, April 1, 1953, to June 30, 1954(?), https://kinginstitute.stanford.edu/king-papers/documents/theology-reinhold-niebuhr-0.

CHAPTER TWO

Hope amid Chaos

Over the course of his pastorate, Reinhold Niebuhr had developed the habit of writing out prayers to accompany his sermons. Although these prayers were often eloquent, the one he wrote for this particular day in the early 1930s was notable for its brevity. "God," he intoned, "give us grace to accept with serenity the things that cannot be changed, courage to change the things that should be changed and the wisdom to distinguish the one from the other." Of all that Niebuhr said or wrote, nothing would enter the spiritual consciousness of American culture quite like the Serenity Prayer. Military chaplains would use it on the battlefields of World War II, and it would become the unofficial mantra of millions of participants in Alcoholics Anonymous programs. Today, it remains one of the most recognizable passages in American letters.[1]

But the Serenity Prayer's legacy in American culture is complex. On the one hand, it has become *so* popular that it is often reduced to little more than a branding tool. We see this in the frequency with which it appears on bracelets, coffee cups, and other mass-produced trinkets. On the other hand, its very ubiquity offers glimpses of its enduring power in unlikely places. Take, for instance, the prayer's popularity as a tattoo. To buy a Serenity Prayer trinket is one thing; to inscribe it permanently on one's flesh is quite another. This suggests that it continues to resonate as a reminder of human frailty and need for God.

Bono, the lead singer of the Irish rock band U2, penned an introduc-

---

1. Fred R. Shapiro, "Who Wrote the Serenity Prayer?" *Chronicle of Higher Education*, April 28, 2014, http://www.chronicle.com/article/Who-Wrote-the -Serenity-Prayer-/146159.

tion to a collection of gospel songs and spirituals sung by legendary country artist Johnny Cash. In it, he explained why songs that could otherwise come off as trite or sentimental retained their spiritual power: "Johnny Cash doesn't sing to the damned, he sings with the damned, and sometimes you feel he might prefer their company."[2] Niebuhr had a similar disposition. He had no tolerance for pious cant, and he took particular delight in religious outsiders finding inspiration in his words. Following a service where Niebuhr preached, Supreme Court justice and lifelong atheist Felix Frankfurter greeted him by saying, "May a believing unbeliever thank you for your sermon?" to which Niebuhr replied, "May an unbelieving believer thank you for appreciating it?"[3] He would have reacted to the Serenity Prayer's mixed legacy along similar lines. Reinhold's daughter, author and editor Elisabeth Sifton, relates that when her father's health flagged later in life, friends would send along "ghastly samples of Serenity Prayer kitsch" to lift his spirits.[4] Although Niebuhr might have smiled wryly at seeing the prayer on a coffee mug or a key chain, he likely took pleasure in hearing it on the lips of the irreverent and the broken.

The decade following the publication of *Moral Man and Immoral Society* marked a crucial turning point for Niebuhr. It was the era in which he rose to national and international prominence, formally broke with pacifism in favor of intervention in World War II, and laid the foundations of the Christian realism that would underlie postwar politics. Yet this period also marks Niebuhr's turn to theology. While Niebuhr's next book, *Reflections on the End of an Era* (1934), is generally remembered for its apocalyptic tone, it is also where he offers his first sustained reflections on the theological themes that would shape his mature thought: sin and grace, the relationship between divine judgment and divine mercy, and how God relates to human affairs. By the time Niebuhr published the second volume of *Nature and Destiny of Man* in 1943, he had established himself as the country's premier theologian. Yet, for all the force and sophistication that Niebuhr's thought acquired during this period, the Serenity Prayer captures the essence of his message.[5] The torrent of

---

2. See insert to Johnny Cash compilation entitled *God* (Sony, 2000).

3. Daniel F. Rice, *Reinhold Niebuhr and His Circle of Influence* (New York: Cambridge University Press, 2013), 206.

4. Elisabeth Sifton, *The Serenity Prayer: Faith and Politics in Times of Peace and War* (New York: Norton, 2005), 295.

5. Andrew Finstuen, *Original Sin and Everyday Protestants* (Chapel Hill: University of North Carolina Press, 2009), 116-17.

sermons, articles, and books that Niebuhr produced in this period was geared to helping others face the uncertainty of the day with serenity, courage, and wisdom.

The 1930s were perhaps the most chaotic decade of the twentieth century. As the world spiraled deeper into an economic depression, fascist movements came to power and attempted world domination. By decade's end World War II was under way. It was only a matter of time before an isolationist United States would be forced to join the bloodiest, farthest-reaching conflict the world had ever seen.

Niebuhr's intellectual development reflected the intensity of these years. In the wake of his disillusion with the Social Gospel, which he had articulated in *Moral Man*, Niebuhr worked furiously to cultivate a theologically grounded approach to the day's urgent political matters. The writings of this period chronicle a process of soul-searching for Niebuhr, as he committed to the notion that Christian concepts of sin, grace, and redemption were rife with implications for how to interpret and respond to the day's chaos. This process eventually led Niebuhr to abandon pacifism in favor of a theologically informed argument for intervention on behalf of the Allied forces in World War II.

Intervention may seem an obvious stance to take in retrospect, but hindsight affords a degree of moral clarity that proves elusive in the heat of the moment. Niebuhr labored hard to articulate a theologically compelling way to break through the isolationist tendencies of a populace too absorbed with domestic problems to seriously consider entering the quagmire of world politics. The product of his efforts, which came to be known as Christian realism, wielded considerable influence once the outcome of the war started to come into focus. Its foundations, however, lay in the 1930s.

Finding a Theological Voice

Niebuhr's transition from insightful critic of liberalism to an original and creative theological voice began in earnest in the wake of an exchange with his brother H. Richard in 1932. With its brisk prose, incisive argumentation, and blistering rhetoric, *Moral Man* had garnered national attention. Yet, with the attention came sharp criticism. Proponents of the Social Gospel across the country perceived his argument as an unfair attack on liberal Christianity that betrayed core elements of the Christian message. For some, his assertion of the inevitability of coercion was not the product of unflinching realism, but rather a symptom of cynicism and despair. This puzzled Social Gospel advocates who had grown to admire the energy and acumen that Niebuhr brought to social justice causes. The reaction of Charles Gilkey, then the dean of Rockefeller Chapel at the University of Chicago Divinity School, summed up these concerns best. His son Langdon recalled how his father retreated into his office with a brand-new copy of *Moral Man* in hand. A couple of hours later, he burst out of his office and exclaimed, "Reinie's gone crazy!"[6] Gary Dorrien observes that to many of Niebuhr's contemporaries, it seemed "that he's denying the gospel itself."

Watching one former collaborator after another join the ranks of his critics took its toll on Reinhold. Likely sensing this discouragement, H. Richard sent his brother a letter congratulating him on the book's success and assuring him of its quality and enduring value. In the letter, H. Richard also ventured his own critique, although from a different perspective. On his reading, the vast majority of criticisms were misplaced. They nearly all asserted that Reinhold had taken his attacks on liberalism too far. H. Richard argued that they had not gone far enough: "You are free from the liberal interpretation of morality—but not quite—and from the liberal interpretation of religion—but not quite. And in that not quite your conflict is based."[7] As H. Richard saw it, the issue was neatly summarized in the book's title. As tough as Reinhold had been on "immoral society," he still held out belief in "moral man." Consequently, he remained "too romantic about human nature in the individual," and thus, was still tethered to the naïve liberalism from which he sought to break free.

H. Richard used a strikingly personal line of argument to expose this latent optimism. He outlined the mix of feelings that he felt toward his brother—pride, jealousy, guilt—as an example of the weakness of human nature. He wrote, "I hate to look at my brotherly love for you. To see how it is compounded with personal pride—I taking some kind of credit for the thing you do and basking in reflected glory—and with selfish ambition—trying to stand on my own feet, trying to live up to you, being jealous of you, to use a harsh and brutal term." H. Richard continued, "If I being evil—in no metaphysical sense—can nevertheless love you it

6. Langdon Gilkey, *On Niebuhr* (Chicago: University of Chicago Press, 2001), 4.
7. This letter may be found in the Reinhold Niebuhr Papers, Library of Congress.

isn't because any ideal or will to love prevails over my putrid instinct & desire—but because something else, which is not my will, was at work long before I had a will or an ideal." In other words, we were not capable of loving even those closest to us of our own accord. We needed an outside force—"something else," H. Richard called it—to overcome our selfish tendencies. And this "something else" contained a pronounced element of coercion: "The apparently more decent behavior of men in face to face relationships is not due at all to any element of reason or of moral idealism, any inclination of the will, but to the fact that there is more coercion . . . and more possibility of identifying ourselves with the other man and loving ourselves in him or her."[8] H. Richard's overarching point was that Reinhold needed to be as tough in his analysis of the individual as he was in his analysis of society. To do this effectively he would need to draw on the vocabulary and insights of theology, particularly the language of sin and grace as Augustine and Reformation-era thinkers such as Luther and Calvin had deployed it. The fourth-century Christian thinker Augustine, as well as those who were influenced by him, argued that the human will was broken, and that outside of the grace of God, humans could do nothing fully good. Although often dismissed as too pessimistic in their assessments of human nature, these thinkers provided the conceptual resources necessary to break definitively with the naïve elements of Social Gospel liberalism.

In effect, H. Richard was saying that despite the international scope of his argument, Reinhold's point of view remained too narrow. While this point of view offered a nuanced account of human interactions, its sense of how the human relationship to God shaped these interactions was underdeveloped. To expand his scope beyond the Social Gospel, Reinhold needed to figure out how to bring the divine/human relationship to bear on his analysis of human affairs. This would require cultivating a theological vocabulary that was largely absent from *Moral Man*.

H. Richard was encouraging Reinhold to appropriate the best of what their ministry-oriented upbringing had to offer. As Healan Gaston notes, the "classic Reformation teachings" of sin and grace were the "centerpiece of what they inherited from their father and what they inherited from their early experiences." The tenor of Reinhold's work over the next

---

8. Reinhold Niebuhr Papers, Library of Congress. Biographer Richard Fox excerpts and analyzes this letter in detail. See Richard Wightman Fox, *Reinhold Niebuhr: A Biography* (Ithaca, NY: Cornell University Press, 1996), 145-46.

decade demonstrates that he took his brother's charge to heart.[9] By the early 1940s Reinhold had cultivated the theologically rich approach to social ethics that would enable him to shape and critique American political and religious discourse for the rest of his career.

Although H. Richard was the catalyst for his brother's theological transformation, Reinhold engaged with other prominent thinkers during this period. Two in particular would prove immensely important to both American and European thought and life: Dietrich Bonhoeffer and Paul Tillich. The facility with German language and culture that Niebuhr had acquired in his youth proved a great asset in his interactions with Bonhoeffer and Tillich, both of whom found the American context disorienting at first.

Dietrich Bonhoeffer

Today Dietrich Bonhoeffer is remembered for the principled and courageous resistance to the Nazi regime that cost him his life. When he arrived at Union in 1930 at the age of twenty-four on a postdoctoral fellowship, he was already establishing himself as one of Europe's brightest theological minds. As Robin Lovin points out, the very fact that Bonhoeffer was at Union at all testified to his brilliance: while he possessed the credentials to serve as a professor in the German university system, he was too young to qualify for a position. This prompted his mentors to make arrangements for him to go to Union for the year.

Life at Union was something of a culture shock to Bonhoeffer. Coming as he did from a formal German academic context, he was taken aback by the comparatively casual nature of faculty-student interaction at the seminary. In the classroom, the method and content departed so markedly from how he had been trained that he found it lacking in theological rigor. As he infamously put it, "there is no theology here."[10]

Bonhoeffer was correct in noting a difference in approach between German universities and Union Seminary. In true Social Gospel fashion, Union emphasized social engagement. This emphasis could (and often did) detract from careful training in Hebrew, Greek, and Latin; from close

---

9. See Fox's analysis of this period in *Reinhold Niebuhr: A Biography*, 142–92.

10. Charles Marsh, *Strange Glory: A Life of Dietrich Bonhoeffer* (New York: Vintage Books, 2015), 104.

readings of biblical and theological texts; and from deep engagement with particular traditions in Christian thought. But while Bonhoeffer found the academic culture of Union wanting, he did learn from its sensitivity to issues of social ethics. On a paper on Martin Luther that Bonhoeffer had written for one of Niebuhr's seminars, Niebuhr reportedly wrote, "There are no ethics here. Where is the ethical dimension in your account? A concept of faith without ethics is an empty concept."[11]

According to biographer Charles Marsh, Bonhoeffer was "mortified" by the critique. Yet it foreshadowed a momentous shift in Bonhoeffer's life and thought. A classmate took him to Abyssinian Baptist Church, a historically black congregation in Harlem. Under the Reverend Adam Clayton Powell Jr., the church brought together religious feeling, social justice, and biblical teaching in a way that left a profound impression on the young German. Five years later Bonhoeffer would write *The Cost of Discipleship*, one of the classic texts in Christian ethics. It is perhaps best remembered for its distinction between a "cheap grace" that requires no substantive change in the individual and the "costly grace" that demands life-transforming obedience to the Christian gospel. Powell used this distinction to critique the inaction of white Christians in the face of the racist atrocities of the Jim Crow era. One also wonders if Niebuhr's criticism helped spur Bonhoeffer's engagement with ethics more generally. Despite his early misgivings, Bonhoeffer's time in New York proved pivotal to his legacy.

Upon completing his year at Union, Bonhoeffer returned to Germany, where he proved instrumental in organizing the Confessing Church in opposition to Hitler. As the situation in Germany deteriorated, Niebuhr helped make arrangements to bring Bonhoeffer back to Union in 1939. But shortly after arriving, Bonhoeffer decided he had to head home. Niebuhr, who as a German American understood the gravity of the situation to which Bonhoeffer was returning, tried to persuade him to stay. But Bonhoeffer was determined. As he wrote to Niebuhr, "I will have no right to participate in the reconstruction of Christian life in Germany after the war if I do not share the trials of this time with my people."[12] He would

---

11. Tiffany Stanley, "The Life of Dietrich Bonhoeffer: An Interview with Charles Marsh," *Religion and Politics*, July 30, 2014, http://religionandpolitics.org/2014/07/30/the-life-of-dietrich-bonhoeffer-an-interview-with-charles-marsh/.

12. Reinhold Niebuhr, "The Death of a Martyr," *Christianity and Crisis* 5, no. 11 (June 25, 1945): 6.

pay the ultimate price for practicing the costly grace that he preached: he was arrested for participating in a foiled assassination attempt on Hitler and was hanged on April 9, 1945, at Flossenbürg concentration camp. In an obituary for Bonhoeffer, Niebuhr noted somberly that his story "belongs to the modern Acts of the Apostles."[13]

Paul Tillich

Reinhold and H. Richard played important roles in bringing another towering figure of twentieth-century thought to American soil from Germany: Paul Tillich. Like the Niebuhr brothers, Tillich was the son of a pastor. He was born in Brandenburg, Germany, in 1886, earned his PhD in 1911, and was ordained a Lutheran minister in 1912. When World War I broke out in 1914, Tillich entered the German army as a military chaplain. Tillich witnessed some of the war's most horrific moments, including the Battle of the Somme—which, with well over one million casualties, ranks among the bloodiest battles in history. This experience rocked him to his core. As historian Andrew Finstuen notes, his intellectual framework was "shattered for him because of what he witnesse[d] in the horrors of trench warfare. Friends, colleagues killed and the utter absurdity and inhumanity of it."[14]

After his discharge from the army in 1918, Tillich moved to Berlin. As he reengaged the academic life, it became clear that his battlefield experience had fundamentally shaped his perspective. Finstuen observes, "On the one hand he has the greatest powers of abstraction and intellectual curiosity. On the other hand he has seen the most raw bloody side of what it means to be human." By the mid-1920s he had gained acclaim for his work at the intersection of philosophy and theology and had been appointed a professor in the German university system.

Like Niebuhr, Tillich spoke out relentlessly on political issues. This cost him his professorship when the Nazis came to power in 1933. The Niebuhr brothers, meanwhile, had become acquainted with Tillich's work on a trip to Germany in 1930, and had grown to admire his thought. H. Richard was impressed enough with Tillich to translate one of his ear-

---

13. Niebuhr, "Death of a Martyr," 6.

14. Journey Films interview with Andrew Finstuen, July 12, 2016. Unless otherwise noted, subsequent quotes attributed to Finstuen are from this interview.

lier works, *The Religious Situation*, into English. Reinhold convinced the Union faculty to take a 5 percent pay cut—during the Great Depression—in order to create a position for Tillich, clearing the way for Tillich to come to the United States in the fall of 1933. Together, Niebuhr and Tillich would set the political and intellectual tone at Union Seminary for the next twenty years.

The two were particularly close in the months immediately following the move. As a German speaker, Niebuhr helped facilitate Tillich's transition to American culture and attempts to improve his English-language skills. Tillich, in turn, helped Niebuhr acquire a distinctive theological voice. For Tillich, theology served the crucial methodological function of relating the eternal realm of the divine to the material world. In so doing, theology helped bridge the chasms between the realm of spirit and the realm of nature, between our inner lives and the world around us. Given this particular understanding of the nature and task of theology, Tillich was especially concerned with issues of epistemology, a branch of philosophy that deals with how human beings acquire and convey knowledge. While Niebuhr lacked Tillich's aptitude for and interest in nuanced, abstract discussion of such things, he found the way that Tillich used theological language compelling. So as Niebuhr helped Tillich navigate life in a new country, Tillich helped accelerate Niebuhr's philosophical and theological development. Fundamental differences would emerge between the two men in the 1940s and 1950s, as later chapters will illustrate. In the early 1930s, however, Tillich's influence on Niebuhr was immense.

Two Starkly Different Works

The two books Niebuhr wrote after *Moral Man* contrast starkly with one another in tone and content. The first of these, *Reflections on the End of an Era* (1934), is widely regarded as Niebuhr's most radical work. It presumes the imminent fall of Western civilization and deploys theological language to salvage a sense of meaning and purpose in the midst of this impending collapse. The following year, 1935, Niebuhr published *An Interpretation of Christian Ethics*, which focuses on how Christianity illumines the spiritual and moral character of human life. Taken together, these books illustrate how Niebuhr assimilated the thought of his two biggest contemporary theological influences. In the preface to *Reflections*,

Niebuhr writes, "I would like to express my gratitude . . . to my brother, Professor H. Richard Niebuhr, who disagrees with most of the conclusions at which I arrive, but whose stimulating analyses of the contemporary religious and social problem prompted many of these reflections."[15] Likewise, in the preface to *Interpretation of Christian Ethics*, Niebuhr notes, "I owe a particular debt of gratitude to my colleague, Professor Paul Tillich, for many valuable suggestions in the development of my theme, some of them made specifically and others the by-product of innumerable discussions on the thesis of this book."[16] H. Richard tellingly compared his brother's thought to a "great iceberg in which three-fourths or more is beneath the surface."[17] Tillich and H. Richard constitute large portions of that iceberg, and in these two books their respective influences break the surface.

Reflections on the End of an Era

> Only a religious individual can lift himself above society without illusion and without despair.
>
> —*Reflections on the End of an Era*

In light of *Moral Man and Immoral Society*'s scathing indictment of liberal naïveté, one might wonder just how much more "radical" Reinhold could get. Yet *Reflections* was radical in a different sense. *Moral Man* had been radical in the sheer vehemence of its reaction to Social Gospel liberalism. But as H. Richard had pointed out, *Moral Man* presumed the morality of the individual in a way that prevented Reinhold from making a clean break from the version of liberalism he rejected. In *Reflections on the End of an Era*, Reinhold demonstrated that he had accepted his brother's critique: he had relinquished his implied faith in the morality of the individual. Instead of seeking to wield coercion in the service of social progress, he now looked to divine grace to supply what was inevitably lacking from human effort. Consequently, Niebuhr's analysis is

---

15. Reinhold Niebuhr, *Reflections on the End of an Era* (New York: Scribner, 1934).

16. Reinhold Niebuhr, *An Interpretation of Christian Ethics* (New York: Harper and Brothers, 1935).

17. Charles W. Kegley and Robert W. Bretall, eds., *Reinhold Niebuhr: His Religious, Social, and Political Thought* (New York: Macmillan, 1956), 97.

unfettered from Social Gospel presuppositions in a way that *Moral Man* was not. It is in this sense that *Reflections* is the more radical work. This more radical approach required Niebuhr to incorporate a new dimension to his big-picture thinking. In addition to using an international perspective to make sense of domestic politics, he now deployed a divine vantage point, a "God's-eye" perspective, to make sense of human events. This brought a theological dimension to his analysis that was largely lacking in *Moral Man*.

A markedly different moral voice emerges as a result of this perspectival shift. In *Moral Man*, Niebuhr had written as a participant in the social struggle; in *Reflections*, he located the struggle in the vast sweep of history. In *Moral Man*, Niebuhr had made it clear who was on the "right" and "wrong" sides of the struggle; in *Reflections*, he pointed out the way that good and evil intermingle in both sides of any given conflict. In *Moral Man*, he had written from the perspective of one who was embedded in the events he described; in *Reflections*, he wrote from the God's-eye perspective of what biographer Richard Wightman Fox calls the "cosmic commentator."[18]

Fox describes Niebuhr's voice from this cosmic vantage point as "Olympian and detached."[19] This could be interpreted to suggest that Niebuhr's God was unconnected to human events—a divine clock maker that set the mechanism of the universe in motion and then left it alone, to borrow a popular image from the European Enlightenment. Niebuhr did indeed have a keen appreciation for divine mystery. As Healan Gaston observes, Niebuhr was aware of God as "transcendent, as potentially inscrutable, as possibly unknowable in certain ways."

Yet Niebuhr was also aware of God as related to human affairs. His conception of grace suggested a distinctly Christian vision in which God's judgment and mercy hover over every moment of history. From a limited human standpoint, we are able to draw distinctions between moral and immoral behavior. But from the standpoint of an all-just and all-knowing God, such distinctions fall away. From the day we are born, we are implicated in the exploitative patterns and structures that pervade all human societies. For that reason alone, we deserve judgment. The very fact that we get to live—let alone thrive—is evidence of unmerited grace and mercy: "The processes of nature and history are revelations

18. Fox, *Reinhold Niebuhr: A Biography*, 151.
19. Fox, *Reinhold Niebuhr: A Biography*, 151.

of grace as well as of judgment. Logically every life deserves destruction. Since it is predatory either individually or collectively, it ought to die at the hands of those it has exploited. Though it may perish in the end, the God of history and nature is truly longsuffering, 'slow to anger and plenteous in mercy.'"[20] Once we see the grace implied in our very existence, we are able to see God's judgment and mercy at work in all of history's ups and downs. This frees us to face the paradoxes of life with both honesty and serenity: "The experience of grace is the apprehension of the absolute from the perspective of the relative.... The world, as it is revealed in the processes of nature, is known to be imperfect and yet it is recognized as a creation of God. Man is regarded as both a sinner and a child of God. In these paradoxes true religion makes present reality bearable even while it insists that God is denied, frustrated, and defied in the immediate situation."[21]

Reflections on the End of an Era is the only major book of Niebuhr's to never be reprinted. This was, in part, because its account of a world fraying at the seams did not resonate in subsequent decades the way it did at the height of the Great Depression. But as Cornel West points out, this is also why *Reflections* is so important: "It's really about the decline and the demise of Capitalist civilization as we know it, owing to escalating levels of corruption, and greed, and cronyism, and nepotism, and narcissism. That could have been written today." Niebuhr's willingness to radically critique his social context prompted no less a critic than theologian Stanley Hauerwas to note, "I miss the Niebuhr of *Reflections at the End of an Era*."[22]

An Interpretation of Christian Ethics

> Faith must feed on reason.... But reason must also feed on faith.
> —*An Interpretation of Christian Ethics*

Having completed his first sustained foray into theology, Niebuhr devoted his next book to developing a Christian ethical vocabulary. He had

20. Niebuhr, *Reflections*, 285.

21. Niebuhr, *Reflections*, 281.

22. Journey Films interview with Stanley Hauerwas, May 24, 2016. Unless otherwise noted, subsequent quotes attributed to Hauerwas are from this interview.

the ideal ally for this project in Paul Tillich, who was now on Union's faculty. Whereas Niebuhr fixed his intellectual gaze outward toward the realms of politics and ethics, Tillich focused on the inner life and the struggle to find meaning and connection with God and with one's fellow humans. Tillich was therefore attuned to the nuances of language and the mechanics of how human beings come to know the world around them in ways that the action-oriented Niebuhr never had been. As Tillich put it many years later, "Niebuhr does not ask, 'How can I know'; he just starts knowing! And he does not ask, 'How could I know,' but leaves the convincing power of his thought without epistemological support."[23]

As Niebuhr immersed himself in theology in the mid-1930s, he seemed to recognize that if he was unwilling to extensively investigate basic philosophical questions about language, knowledge, and God, he should at least pay close attention to the work of those who had. As he set about assembling the manuscript of *An Interpretation of Christian Ethics*, he reportedly brought a stack of Tillich's writings with him. It is unsurprising then that, as Fox observes, "Tillich's vocabulary shone from virtually every page."[24] Whereas *Reflections* developed a God's-eye perspective on human events, *Interpretations* focused once again on the spirituality and ethics of individuals. Human beings, Niebuhr argued, are not content merely to exist; they must also be able to experience their existence as meaningful. To find meaning, they must have access to vocabulary that accounts for the heights and depths of human experience — a task for which purely rational language is ill-suited. To apprehend life in all its "richness and contradictoriness," and to stake out the ethical terrain on which such a life plays out, one needs access to the "mythic" language of religion.

The term "myth" is often used as a synonym for fable, or to describe a story as untrue or unreal. For Niebuhr, however, "myth" describes language that relates the time-bound to the eternal and the finite to the infinite. Myth, in other words, was that category of language that enabled us to understand God and humanity as related. For language to accomplish this purpose, it had to take us beyond the rules of rational consistency. By way of analogy, Niebuhr compares a portrait to a photograph: "In the latter the immediate actualities are faithfully and accurately recorded;

---

23. Paul Tillich, "Reinhold Niebuhr's Doctrine of Knowledge," in Kegley and Bretall, *Reinhold Niebuhr: His Religious, Social, and Political Thought*, 35-54.
24. Fox, *Reinhold Niebuhr: A Biography*, 161.

but the mood of the moment which the photograph catches may obscure or falsify the quintessential spirit of a personality. The portrait artist, on the other hand, will falsify, unduly accentuate, and select physiognomic details in order to present his vision of the transcendent unity and spirit of the personality."[25] Just as a skilled portrait artist must adjust proportion, lighting, and texture to represent the subject in a way that captures the subject's personality, to capture human experience in its totality we must deploy imagery, symbolism, and allegory and other modes of language that enable us to transition from literal to mythic understandings of the world.[26]

As frustrating as religion's deployment of mythic language might be to those who want all truth to reflect the precision and coherence of pure reason, for Niebuhr a morally satisfying account of the world was impossible without myth. Just as God transcends reason, so do aspects of the human spirit. To describe ourselves in relation to reality in a comprehensive sense, we must be willing to use language that transports us beyond rational limits. In a Christian context, we need stories such as the account of the fall of humanity in Genesis, dense symbols such as the cross of Christ, and Gospel depictions of a cosmic final judgment to articulate the ecstasies and agonies of our inner lives, account for the human experience of good and evil, and cultivate an ethical vision of a just society. Without access to mythic language capable of relating the finite to the eternal, this sort of robust description of human experience would be impossible.

An Interpretation of Christian Ethics, then, was meant to help individuals to locate themselves within the God's-eye view of human affairs as outlined in *Reflections on the End of an Era*. In *Reflections*, Niebuhr had taught his readers to see sin and grace, divine judgment and divine mercy at work in history. In *Interpretation* he encouraged his readers to see these theological categories at work in their inner lives and daily interactions. In tandem, these books presented Niebuhr's vision for how God's relationship with humanity plays out both in the inner life of individuals and in the arena of human relations. Niebuhr was now ready to bring his theologically informed perspective to bear on the pressing political, philosophical, and ethical issues of the day.

25. Niebuhr, *Interpretation of Christian Ethics*, 83.
26. For a nuanced treatment of the strengths and weaknesses of the portrait/photograph analogy, see Fox, *Reinhold Niebuhr: A Biography*, 162-63.

Life outside the Seminary

Earning a full-time appointment to Union's faculty did little to hamper Niebuhr's extraordinarily active life beyond the seminary's walls, both as a preacher and as an activist. As was true during his years in Detroit, he was in high demand as a speaker and a preacher. Students recall that it was common for Niebuhr to show up to teach with a suitcase in hand and dash off to catch the next train as soon as class ended.

Niebuhr does not appear to have preached any less once he left Bethel: he simply exchanged one pulpit for many. Chapel services, usually sparsely attended, were filled to capacity when Niebuhr came to speak. Looking back on this period, Niebuhr described himself as a circuit rider, in the fashion of preachers that would travel from town to town on the nineteenth-century frontier.[27] In the age of mass transit, Niebuhr covered a vast area, traversing the Northeast, the mid-Atlantic, and the Midwest.

What was peculiar about Niebuhr's circuit is that it consisted almost entirely of university and seminary chapels rather than churches. Reinhold's daughter Elisabeth recalls that there were "two churches, possibly three, in the whole United States that asked him to come and preach." The country's religious establishment wanted nothing to do with Niebuhr or his message: "Most congregations and most pastors and priests and vicars in the American church did not want to hear his upsetting analysis of the ills of the American community and did not want to encourage him to sound off about the blatant discrimination and injustice that he could see all around him—they didn't want to hear that." For those with ears to hear, however, Niebuhr's sermons could shatter paradigms. Arthur Schlesinger Jr., the historian, adviser to John F. Kennedy, and influential political consultant, heard Niebuhr preach while he was a student at Harvard. The language with which Schlesinger described Niebuhr in the pulpit is reminiscent of how Ishmael described Father Mapple's sermon in chapter 9 of Herman Melville's classic novel *Moby Dick*: "Establishing instant command over the congregation, he spoke, without notes, in rushes of jagged eloquence. His eyes flashed; his voice rose and sank to a whisper . . . but underneath the dramatics, his argument was cool, rigorous, and powerful. Man was flawed and sinful, he told an initially

---

27. Kegley and Bretall, *Reinhold Niebuhr: His Religious, Social, and Political Thought*, 3.

dubious congregation. Yet even sinful man had the duty of acting against evil in the world."[28]

Various others were similarly moved upon hearing Niebuhr speak. Elisabeth Sifton relates a conversation she had with the late William Bundy, a CIA intelligence expert and foreign policy adviser during the Kennedy and Johnson administrations, in which he recalled hearing Niebuhr speak at Yale during his days as a student in the 1930s. At the time, "Yale was kind of isolationist America-firsters who did not want anything to do with what was roiling waters in Europe—they didn't want to hear about fascism on the rise." Then along came Niebuhr, making a case for interventionism from the university chapel's pulpit. As Bundy described it, "I heard your father preach and relate all those non-spoken things to the Gospel—I'll tell you, it knocked my socks off." These stories confirm what many have claimed: as compelling as Niebuhr could be in print, he was most in his element as a preacher. Elisabeth agreed with her mother: "The spoken word was his art form."

Although Niebuhr was more immersed in theology in this period than he had ever been, he remained engaged in activism. This exposed him to the societal issues that gave his sermons their conscience-rousing power. In 1936 he served as chairman for the first board of trustees for the Delta Cooperative Farm, an integrated group of black and white families in Hillhouse, Mississippi. The project was remarkable in its attempt to provide sound economic foundations for racial justice projects in the Jim Crow South. Shortly after its founding, Niebuhr called it "the most significant social experiment now being conducted in America."[29] Professor emeritus and former Niebuhr graduate assistant Ronald Stone notes that Niebuhr "was particularly complimented for being the one who could arrange the compromises that were needed to keep the farm together."[30] A number of Delta Cooperative members enlisted to fight in World War II, which prompted a merger with nearby Providence Cooperative Farm in 1942. The Providence Farm closed in the mid-1950s, due in large part to the toxic race politics and "red scare" paranoia about the "communist overtones" of cooperative endeavors that characterized

---

28. Arthur Schlesinger Jr., *A Life in the Twentieth Century: Innocent Beginnings, 1917-1950* (New York: Houghton Mifflin, 2000), 249.

29. Fox, *Reinhold Niebuhr: A Biography*, 176.

30. Journey Films interview with Ronald Stone, April 12, 2016. Unless otherwise noted, subsequent quotes attributed to Stone are from this interview.

the era. However, the fact that such an integrated cooperative existed at all—let alone that it managed to continue for two decades—is astonishing. Niebuhr saw clearly that economic and race issues were intimately linked: they needed to be addressed simultaneously. He was willing to invest time, energy, and resources into communities that sought to fuse economic and racial justice.

The Delta Cooperative Farm arguably marked the apex of Niebuhr's involvement on issues of race. As theologian James Cone argues, "Niebuhr's work with his theological admirers and former students in the Delta ministry was . . . perhaps, the only time he would engage the black struggle for justice."[31] We will examine the issue of Niebuhr on race in greater detail in chapter 5, when we turn to civil rights. For now, it is enough to note that from the late 1930s onward Niebuhr ceased to be as intellectually invested in cooperative movements, in part because he did not think they could ultimately bring about the systemic changes necessary to advancing the cause of justice. Ronald Stone observes, "Niebuhr believed in cooperative movements and energetically worked with them but he knew that wasn't where the rubber hit the road. . . . If you were going to reform that agricultural system or racial relations . . . you need to enlist the power of government." While grassroots cooperatives were "good as demonstrative models," meaningful structural change happened from the top down. Stone concludes, "critics who say of Niebuhr that he's government- or state-oriented are correct—he believed [that] to cause real social change you [need] power, money, [and] possibilities of institutional dependency which you can count on." The efforts of the cooperative, however, just may have succeeded in inspiring important top-down change. Biographer Paul Merkley noted that there is "some supporting evidence" for the view that the Delta Cooperative "provided inspiration for several of the experiments in community rescue that Franklin Roosevelt undertook in the later years of the New Deal."[32]

Following the launch of the Delta Cooperative, Niebuhr's attention began to turn back to international affairs and academic pursuits. In the summer of 1937, he headed to England to participate in the Oxford Conference on Church, Community, and State, which brought together Protestant church leaders from around the world. Niebuhr was asked to

---

31. James H. Cone, *The Cross and the Lynching Tree* (Maryknoll, NY: Orbis, 2011), 45.
32. Paul Merkley, *Reinhold Niebuhr: A Political Account* (Montreal: McGill-Queens University Press, 1975), 256.

deliver the Oxford conference's keynote address. With his frenetic energy, pragmatic approach, and penchant for speaking his mind, Niebuhr brought a distinctly American voice to the proceedings. Geared as it was toward a society in disarray, Niebuhr's message resonated with an audience struggling to come to terms with the social turbulence they witnessed around them. As Anglican Archbishop William Temple put it when introduced to Niebuhr, "At last I have met the disturber of my peace."[33]

Niebuhr later edited his address, publishing it as "The Christian Church in a Secular Age." Given the worsening political conditions on the European continent, this article was striking in how it emphasized theological concepts of sin, divine judgment, and divine mercy over incisive political commentary. Niebuhr, however, had grown to realize that these concepts brimmed with political implications. The Christian gospel, Niebuhr reminded us, "does not abstract us from the present history with all of its conflicts and tragic disappointments of arrogant hopes. We are in the world, and God's will, His Judgment and His Mercy impinge upon our daily actions and historic problems."[34] It is in apprehending the gospel that we are able to "understand life in all its beauty and its terror, without being beguiled by its beauty or driven to despair by its terror."[35] Taking the insights of Christian thought seriously is key to navigating the chaos of the present.

In this piece we sense Niebuhr's determination to bring a God's-eye view to bear on the deeply troubling political developments that so weighed on the minds of conference participants. When we keep in mind that all events transpire under the gaze of a just, merciful, and all-knowing God, we are able to approach even the most difficult circumstances with clarity of judgment and serenity of disposition. And Niebuhr remained as committed as he had ever been to political engagement. As Stone points out, Niebuhr "would've agreed with Aristotle: If you're not political, you're either an idiot or a god." Theology serves the crucial political function of helping us make sense of and respond to events unfolding around us. In his hands, faith and activism are not separate

33. Fox, *Reinhold Niebuhr: A Biography*, 180.

34. Elisabeth Sifton, ed., *Reinhold Niebuhr: Major Works* (New York: Library of America, 2015), 736.

35. Sifton, *Reinhold Niebuhr: Major Works*, 736.

spheres: rather, faith spurs and deepens activism, and activism enables faith to touch down in everyday life.

Beyond Tragedy

Man is mortal. That is his fate. Man pretends not to be mortal. That is his sin.

—Beyond Tragedy

After publishing "The Christian Church in a Secular Age," Niebuhr reflected further on the implications of the Oxford conference in an additional set of writings. In the fall of 1937 Niebuhr published *Beyond Tragedy*, a collection of sermons on various themes raised at the Oxford conference. H. Richard loved this particular collection, calling it the "best theology which has appeared in America in a generation or two." While this praise was arguably a bit effusive in light of the contributions of Social Gospel pioneer Walter Rauschenbusch (or even H. Richard himself), this was certainly Niebuhr's most theologically complete work to date: "There is more positive assurance," the younger Niebuhr noted, "more faith, hope and love in this book than anything I've seen in a long time."[36]

The notion of "positive assurance" points to the constructive nature of the work: Reinhold was offering an alternative to the naïve Social Gospel liberalism he had eviscerated in *Moral Man*. That H. Richard described the book as containing "faith, hope and love"—traditionally regarded as the three theological virtues—suggests the coherence of the theological worldview underpinning these essays. Since they originated as sermons, these essays retained something of the dynamism with which he was able to infuse the spoken word. As H. Richard noted, "It's amazing how many ideas you are able to pack into a paragraph or a section."[37] Niebuhr's flare as a preacher was on full display as he layered image upon image to expound on themes drawn from biblical passages.

As the title of the collection hints, *Beyond Tragedy* was where Reinhold finally struck the balance between facing the tragic element in human life and insisting that this tragic element did not have the final say. In Reinhold's hands, theological language was deployed both to *confront*

36. Fox, *Reinhold Niebuhr: A Biography*, 184.
37. Reinhold Niebuhr Papers, Library of Congress.

tragedy in its full dimensions and to articulate a way *beyond* tragedy. Mark Massa explains the intuition behind Niebuhr's approach: "the first thing you have to realize is you cannot save yourself, and you're going to hell in a handbasket, and that's good news because God's grace can save us from that."

While Reinhold had been building on H. Richard's insight for several years, in *Beyond Tragedy* the various aspects of his theology began to cohere. He brought together the God's-eye view of *Reflections on the End of an Era* with the human's-eye view of being confronted with sin and grace articulated in *An Interpretation of Christian Ethics*. Both perspectives are evident in Niebuhr's prefatory remarks:

> It is the thesis of these essays that the Christian view of history passes through the sense of the tragic to a hope and an assurance which is "beyond tragedy." The cross, which stands at the center of the Christian worldview, reveals both the seriousness of human sin and the purpose and power of God to overcome it. It reveals man violating the will of God in his highest moral and spiritual achievements . . . and God absorbing evil into Himself in the very moment of its most vivid expression. Christianity's view of history is tragic insofar as it recognizes evil as the inevitable concomitant of even the highest spiritual enterprises. It is beyond tragedy inasfar as it does not regard evil as inherent in existence itself but as finally under the dominion of a good God.[38]

In a chapter entitled "The Tower of Babel," Niebuhr used a single image to explore how the divine/human relationship informs human affairs. Genesis 11 tells the story of how humanity chose to build a "tower with its top in the heavens" in order to "make a name for ourselves." Upon seeing the tower, God came down and confused the language of the builders so that they could no longer communicate. The passage concludes, "there the LORD confused the language of all the earth; and from there the LORD scattered them abroad over the face of all the earth" (Gen. 11:1-9).

For Niebuhr, this story described a key element of the human experience. Our efforts to "make a name for ourselves" in history are ultimately frustrated because our attempts to build monuments to our own greatness presuppose a degree of dominion over the world that we simply do

---

38. Reinhold Niebuhr, *Beyond Tragedy* (New York: Scribner, 1937), x-xi. Hereafter, page references from this work will be given in parentheses in the text.

not have. However benign and passive our existence might seem on the surface, in the mere act of belonging to a civilization we become complicit in building towers of Babel: "True religion [displays] a profound uneasiness about our highest social values. Its uneasiness springs from the knowledge that the God whom it worships transcends the limits of finite man, while this same man is constantly tempted to forget the finiteness of his cultures and civilization and to pretend a finality for them which they do not have. Every civilization and every culture is thus a Tower of Babel" (28).

Our drive to build such towers was rooted in the fact that we possessed the potential for true greatness. Indeed, it was precisely this greatness that drove humanity to reach beyond what it could achieve, to try to compete with divine boundlessness through finite human works: "Man touches the fringes of the eternal and universal. Only because he has this dignity can he be tempted to exceed his bounds and claim for the achievements of his spirit a universality which they can never possess" (43). Every artifact of human civilization aspires in some way to this false permanence: "Every form of human culture, whether religious, rational, or scientific, is subject to the same corruption, because all are products of the same human heart, which tries to deny its finite limitations" (38).

It may be tempting to see God's disruption of Babel's construction by confounding human language as an unfair punishment. But Niebuhr argued that a closer reading of the Babel story revealed this punishment to be an act of mercy. The difficulties and frustrations that the array of languages introduced into human life remind us that "the highest pinnacles of the human spirit lie grounded in contingencies of nature and history" (42). Similarly, when we confront the inevitable decline of our civilizations, we are reminded of our limits and presented with an opportunity to repent, to recognize that only God possesses ultimate power and eternal grace. While this repentance would not necessarily "save the enterprises of collective man from the periodic catastrophes that overtake them," it instills in us the humility necessary to build anew (45).

In Niebuhr's hands, the Tower of Babel motif became a basis for understanding the interplay of sin and redemption in history. We build great things because we "touch the fringes of the eternal." What we build will collapse, because we inevitably try to transcend our limits. We find the impetus to build again, because we are capable of repenting of our hubris. History thus reveals the corruption in our most sublime achievements and the mercy available to us in their collapse. From American radio shows to European lecture halls, Niebuhr spent the next few years using this integrated perspective to bring analytical clarity and moral urgency to the increasingly dire geopolitical situation of the late 1930s and early 1940s.

The Gifford Lectures

Following the publication of *Beyond Tragedy*, Niebuhr began preparations to deliver the Gifford Lectures, which he had been invited to deliver in Edinburgh, Scotland, in 1939. He was only the fifth American to be invited to participate in the lecture series. For Robin Lovin, this invitation serves as evidence that "other people took Reinhold Niebuhr more seriously as a theologian than he took himself": whereas Niebuhr saw himself primarily as a social ethicist concerned with how to build a more just society, he was coming to be regarded as a theological "force to be reckoned with."

Even during his most intense period of intellectual immersion in preparation for the lectures, he routinely left the ivory tower to engage with the broader political realm. In February of 1939 Niebuhr appeared on *America's Town Meeting of the Air*, a live radio broadcast geared toward current events. His ten-minute speech is among the earliest extant audio clips of Niebuhr's public speaking. In familiar fashion he argued that humanity had put too much trust in technological solutions to modern problems and had underestimated the sheer capacity for self-destruction that human beings possessed. In the hands of immensely creative yet sinful human beings, technological advances increased the human capacity for evil as well as for good. Niebuhr used strikingly contemporary references to make the point: "The radio spreads such enlightened words as I am now speaking to millions," he said in a tone of mock self-importance. "But it also . . . becomes the perfect tool of [Nazi propaganda minister] Dr. Goebbels' ministry of lies. The airplane, about which naïve idealists were certain would increase mutuality . . . has become the most powerful tool of international conflict. The threat of destruction from the air is the nightmare of Europe."

While Niebuhr stopped short of advocating for American intervention, he was clearly determined to make sure that the United States paid close attention to what was happening in Europe. Remaining aloof from the unfolding chaos was simply not an option. The question was not *if*

America would get involved, but *how*: Could the United States devise nonmilitary means of helping to stop the spread of fascism, or was military intervention the only viable option left? Niebuhr found himself struggling to maintain two increasingly contradictory stances: a commitment to pacifism and a commitment to political engagement. Following the First World War, holding both positions seemed straightforward enough. Even after he acknowledged the need for coercion to bring about social change in *Moral Man*, the possibility remained that nonviolent methods could provide sufficiently potent coercive mechanisms. But world politics were straining to the breaking point Niebuhr's ability to hold both positions.

These questions loomed large as Niebuhr made his way to Scotland that spring to deliver his first set of Gifford Lectures. These lectures were arguably the most prestigious showcase in the world for scholars of religion. They were also steeped in European formality: they were typically read from meticulously crafted transcripts. Yet this self-proclaimed "yahoo from Missouri" delivered the lectures, not with polished manuscripts, but with skeleton outlines.

This is not to say that Niebuhr was unprepared. Since receiving the invitation in 1937, he had immersed himself in the works of the most sophisticated philosophical and theological minds in Western thought, from Plato and Aristotle up through Nietzsche and Freud. But after decades of preaching and lecturing from outlines, he saw no need to revise his methods. His dynamic style and reputation for articulating the relevance of even the most seemingly arcane theological concepts to contemporary problems piqued the curiosity of the locals, who filled Rainy Hall at the University of Edinburgh to hear him speak.

The Nature and Destiny of Man

Human Nature

Man has always been his own most vexing problem.

— *The Nature and Destiny of Man*

With titles such as "Man as a Problem to Himself," "The Easy Conscience of Modern Man," and "Original Sin and Man's Responsibility," Niebuhr's first set of lectures established his understanding of human nature. As spirit-animal hybrids, human beings are perched precariously between the realm of nature and the realm of spirit. On the one hand, humans are subject to the same basic strictures as other mammals: they eat, drink, sleep, copulate, defecate, and eventually die. On the other hand, they are spiritual beings made in God's image. They possess powers of reason, fertile imaginations, hopes, and dreams that push them to transform the world as they find it. Human beings, therefore, are both radically limited and radically free. In a basic sense, all moral questions consist in bringing our animal needs and spiritual capacities into balance.

Niebuhr argued that we find this balance when we take responsibility over that which we can control and trust God with the things that we cannot. However, bringing limitation and freedom into equilibrium is an anxiety-inducing process, in part because our limitations imply a lack of control over our own fate. Even our most careful plans can backfire in unpredictable ways. The account of the Fall in Genesis demonstrates that we inevitably cope with this anxiety by taking matters into our own hands. Just as Adam and Eve partook of the fruit from the tree of knowledge of good and evil on the false promise that once they did they would "be as gods," we grasp for a degree of control over our own fate that our creaturely limitations simply cannot sustain. Original sin describes the inevitability with which we seek to control what God alone can.

Niebuhr insisted that, while original sin was inevitable, it wasn't necessary. This may seem like a needlessly fussy distinction, but for Niebuhr it was crucial. To say that we *necessarily* sin implies that sin compromises moral freedom in a way that relieves us of ethical responsibility. But Niebuhr insisted that we remain fully responsible for our moral failings precisely because we remain radically free. We sin, in other words, because we refuse to trust God to sustain us in both our finitude and our freedom. While we can't overcome our moral failings without divine grace, we remain capable of repenting for our sins, receiving forgiveness, and learning to trust. The inevitability with which we sin does not alter this capacity. This formulation of original sin aligned more with nineteenth-century Danish existentialist philosopher Søren Kierkegaard, who rooted his understanding of original sin in the experience of anxiety, than it did with Augustine, who had argued that original sin was sexually transmitted, and thus marked human development from the moment of conception.

That Niebuhr enthralled his audiences does not necessarily imply that they understood him. The sheer speed with which he spoke and the way in which he layered ideas and images on one another could make him difficult to follow. As Healan Gaston describes it, Niebuhr had a "tumbling mind. Ideas just tumbled out of him, faster sometimes than he could even put into words." But Niebuhr's body language and presence in a room communicated his message in ways that transcended the words themselves. A Scotswoman from the audience of one of his lectures put it best: "I dinna understand a word ye say when ye preach, but somehow I ken that you're makin' God great."[39]

Niebuhr spent the summer months following the first round of lectures traveling across the European continent for various speaking engagements. By the time he returned to Edinburgh in October, Great Britain had declared war on Germany; Germany responded by initiating aerial attacks on Britain, starting with Scotland. One lecture was even interrupted by the sound of bombs. Biographer Richard Wightman Fox describes the scene: "German planes were hitting a base a few miles away, and his listeners began to grow restive at the sound of anti-aircraft guns. Niebuhr was so wrapped up in his message that he heard nothing; he thought they were squirming about something he had said."[40] Yet, even under these circumstances, the lecture hall continued to fill. After all, "these were not standard Gifford lectures; they were inspirational if sometimes dense sermons on the Christian view of human destiny," delivered by a master preacher.[41] At a time when this destiny seemed particularly fragile, Niebuhr provided both an unsparing assessment of human nature and a radically hopeful trust in God's greatness.

Human Destiny

Thus the present must wait upon the future for its fulfillment.

— *The Nature and Destiny of Man*

The picture that Niebuhr drew of human destiny was less developed than his depiction of human nature, in part because, in his framework, destiny and faith were closely connected. For Niebuhr, we could live up to our

39. Fox, *Reinhold Niebuhr: A Biography*, 188.
40. Fox, *Reinhold Niebuhr: A Biography*, 191.
41. Fox, *Reinhold Niebuhr: A Biography*, 191.

destiny only by trusting a God beyond our comprehension with a future that we could not foresee. He took to heart the biblical admonition,

> My thoughts are not your thoughts,
>> nor are your ways my ways, says the LORD. (Isa. 55:8)

However, we *were* able to understand the posture toward God and toward one another that would free us to fulfill this destiny; Niebuhr focused his analysis accordingly.

Our ability to glimpse human destiny is tied to the hope of resurrection. In Christian teaching, at time's end there will be a last judgment in which all of humanity will give account before God. This event is often associated with the fate of individual souls: whether one will be deemed worthy of heaven or condemned to hell. Yet Niebuhr pointed out that the last judgment also implied the redemption of history itself. Societies, after all, are composed of individuals who over a lifetime of experiencing birth and death, family, friendship, and conflict become linked to one another in an array of complicated ways. For Niebuhr, belief in an afterlife in which human *individuals* were redeemed presupposed that human *relationships* were redeemed as well. And at their core, human societies were vast and intricate webs of relationships. The hope of resurrection, then, is to assert the ultimate meaningfulness of human events: "The idea of the resurrection implies that the historical elaborations of the richness of creation, in all their variety, will participate in the consummation of history. It gives the struggles in which men engaged to preserve civilizations, and to fulfill goodness in history, abiding significance and does not relegate them to a meaningless flux, of which there will be no echo in eternity."[42] The hope of the resurrection means that human history is not simply a series of fleeting, unrelated, random events. Rather, resurrection makes human history part of God's grand plan to redeem the entire created world.

We see hints of this at work in our experience of grace as God's power within, and God's mercy over, human beings. We see God's grace at work as a *power within* human beings whenever they enact good in the world in a nonegocentric way. When we succeed at "organizing life from beyond the center of the self," the "fruits of grace" are always in-

---

42. Reinhold Niebuhr, *The Nature and Destiny of Man* (New York: Scribner, 1943), 312.

volved.[43] Thanks to the work of grace within us, we can begin to learn to trust God and one another.

The fact that our relationships will be redeemed does not mean that we experience them that way in the here and now. The world remains broken. And while we begin to see evidence of the work of grace in ourselves and others, we remain trapped in sinful patterns of selfishness and mistrust. We experience God's grace as *mercy over* us whenever we come to terms with the fact that we are forgiven and loved even when we are at our worst. Grace thus manifests as unmerited (and thus merciful) forgiveness that covers over our sins even as grace operates in us to spur us toward good. Through openness to both forms of grace, we find the resources that we need to strive for good in our particular historical context despite our inevitable failures: "The two sides of the experience of grace are so related that they do not contradict, but support each other. To understand that Christ in us is not a possession but a hope, that perfection is not a reality but an intention; that such peace as we know in this life is never purely the peace of achievement but the serenity of being 'completely known and all forgiven'; all this does not destroy moral ardor or responsibility."[44] This combination of present receptivity to grace and future hope in resurrection enables us to embrace our destiny as children of God: "Thus wisdom about our destiny is dependent upon a humble recognition of the limits of our knowledge and our power. Our most reliable understanding is the fruit of 'grace' in which faith completes our ignorance without pretending to possess its certainties as knowledge; and in which contrition mitigates our pride without destroying our hope."[45] Acquiring this wisdom requires us to go against the grain of our natural inclinations. We are inclined to transcend our limits, not accept them; this is why Adam and Eve partook of the tree of knowledge in defiance of God's command. In learning to accept our limits, we begin to address the damage done by sin. We learn to manage the knowledge gained through defying our limits by means of the wisdom gained by accepting them.

The Nature and Destiny of Man marks Niebuhr's most comprehensive and sustained foray into theology. It is also where we see Niebuhr thinking about human community in more nuanced and hopeful terms. Ethicist Lisa Cahill points out that Niebuhr repeatedly invoked the phrase

---

43. Niebuhr, *Nature and Destiny*, 123.
44. Niebuhr, *Nature and Destiny*, 125.
45. Niebuhr, *Nature and Destiny*, 321.

"structures of brotherhood," which describes human communities "in their capacity to be bearers of justice and encouragers of just behavior."[46] This is a marked contrast from earlier work. In *Moral Man* there is little, if any, sense of the potential good within human communities. But as Cahill explains, in *Nature and Destiny* Niebuhr recognizes that communities can be bearers of the "positive potential of grace in history."

On balance, the lectures represent the completion of a process rather than the breaking of new intellectual ground. The process began with H. Richard's letter following the publication of *Moral Man*. Healan Gaston observes that H. Richard spurred Reinhold's theological development throughout the 1930s, and concludes that "in some respects *The Nature and Destiny of Man* is the culmination of all that prodding from H. Richard."

A Plea for Intervention

Niebuhr returned from England with renewed appreciation for how dire the political situation in Europe had become, and was more determined than ever to make the case for US intervention. As much as he valued pacifism as an ideal, he dreaded the sort of world that might emerge if fascism was victorious. He broke with pacifist politics in a 1940 article fittingly titled "An End to Illusions." In it, he made public his decision to resign from the Socialist Party because he refused to toe the neutralist party line. "The Socialists have a dogma that this war is a clash of rival imperialisms," he wrote. "Of course they are right. So is a clash between myself and a gangster a conflict of rival egotisms."[47] The pacifist stance that the Socialist Party sought to preserve through neutrality failed to take into account that there was no way to remain untainted by the "rough stuff of politics."[48] He concluded, "If Hitler is to be defeated in the end it will be because the crisis has awakened in us the will to preserve a civilization in which justice and freedom are realities, and given us the knowledge that ambiguous methods are required for the ambiguities of history. Let

---

46. Journey Films interview with Lisa Cahill, May 31, 2016. Unless otherwise noted, subsequent quotes attributed to Cahill are from this interview.

47. Reinhold Niebuhr, "An End to Illusions," in Sifton, *Reinhold Niebuhr: Major Works*, 620.

48. Sifton, *Reinhold Niebuhr: Major Works*, 622.

those who are revolted by such ambiguities have the decency and consistency to retire to the monastery, where medieval perfectionists found their asylum."[49] While this article was political in content, the theology underpinning it was clear: the world is fallen, and human beings are sinful. Under such conditions, we are sometimes forced to make decisions between the lesser of two evils. As reprehensible as killing other human beings might be, there are times where war is the lesser evil. Such are the tragic realities of a sin-ridden world.

There was considerably more subtlety to Niebuhr's thought than this article reflects, but 1940 was hardly the time for nuanced argument. It is easy to overlook in retrospect how strong a force isolationism was in American politics at the time. By way of illustration: in May of 1939 the Roosevelt administration refused to allow the German Jewish immigrants who were aboard the *St. Louis* to disembark in Miami, even though the alternative was for the ship to head back to Nazi Germany. The US government was more concerned with avoiding any action that would be perceived as nudging the country toward war than with sparing the lives of refugees. Isolationism was having concrete geopolitical consequences, and pacifist arguments were often invoked as moral justification for keeping isolationist policies in place.

Against this backdrop, Niebuhr made his next appearance on the *Town Meeting of the Air*, on May 8, 1941. The conversation was shrouded in tension. The day's discussion was entitled "Should Our Ships Convoy Materials to England?" Niebuhr debated John T. Flynn, a founding member of the America First Committee, which opposed involvement in World War II and had eight hundred thousand members at its peak. Both men expressed concern over Hitler's growing power, and both realized that a convoy would substantially increase the likelihood of the United States being dragged into the conflict. In his opening remarks Flynn cited a Gallup poll that indicated 80 percent of Americans were opposed to entering the war. Niebuhr countered by arguing that churches should support Allied victory, thereby implying that, irrespective of public sentiment, getting involved in the war effort was morally preferable to isolationism. This particular *Town Meeting* episode proved memorable enough to be selected for inclusion in the Library of Congress's National Recording Registry in 2009.[50]

---

49. Sifton, *Reinhold Niebuhr: Major Works*, 623.
50. The National Recording Registry's summary of the exchange is available at:

The Japanese attack on Pearl Harbor on December 7, 1941, rendered the interventionist-isolationist debate moot. The United States declared war on Japan the following day, and on Germany a few days after that. The United States was now fully invested in the conflict. As the war escalated, many of those who sought to make sense of the carnage engulfing the globe found a guiding light in Niebuhr. His case for intervention—which months earlier seemed alarmist and morally suspect to his critics—now sounded prescient. To the average American, newsstand headlines across the country verified Niebuhr's claim that original sin made its presence felt in "every moment of existence" and on "every page of human history."[51] Niebuhr's life and thought pointed the way to salvaging hope and finding the strength to act decisively amid the ruins of a deeply broken world. The words that American troops prayed on the battlefield found new resonance on the home front as well: "God, give us grace to accept with serenity the things that cannot be changed, courage to change the things that should be changed and the wisdom to distinguish the one from the other."

---

https://www.loc.gov/programs/static/national-recording-preservation-board/documents/AMERICA'S%20TOWN%20MEETING.pdf.
51. Niebuhr, *Interpretation of Christian Ethics*, 88–90.

CHAPTER THREE

Visions of a New World Order

G ray-black storm clouds swirl in the background. Between the roiling heavens and a dark patch of earth stands a small, shining cross. In the foreground a somber figure gazes off into the distance, his brow furrowed in contemplation as he surveys—well, the viewer can only guess. The atmospherics suggest a tumultuous scene: a battlefield, perhaps, or the wreckage of a bombed-out city. The caption underneath reads "Reinhold Niebuhr: Man's story is not a success story."

The scene conjures up a medieval hellscape—not the usual fare for a magazine cover. Covers, after all, are designed to entice the viewer into purchasing the product: hence, the faces of the beautiful, the notorious, and the powerful monopolize magazine stands. But March of 1948 was no ordinary time. The world had scarcely begun to assess the carnage of world war when a new confrontation among superpowers began to emerge. In March of 1946 Winston Churchill delivered his iconic "Iron Curtain" speech decrying the incursion of the Soviet Union into Eastern Europe. In July of 1947 George Kennan, an American diplomat fresh from an assignment to the Soviet Union, published the famous "Mr. X" article, which outlined the strategy of containment that would dominate US Cold War foreign policy. Rumors circulated that the Soviet Union was on the brink of having an atom bomb. With the specter of nuclear confrontation looming, "Man's story is not a success story" seemed less a needlessly dour pronouncement and more a statement of painfully obvious fact.

Perhaps the cover did not appear as foreboding to its intended audience as it does to us. The shining cross, for instance, could be read as a symbol of hope. And few had worked as tirelessly to snatch hope from the jaws of despair as Reinhold Niebuhr. While others were still speculating about the war's outcome, Niebuhr was envisioning what postwar collaboration would look like in the wake of Allied victory. His 1944 book *The Children of Light and the Children of Darkness* presented a template for democracy in the postwar context and outlined a vision for building world community. He refused to let the gloom of the present rob Americans of hope for the future.

As the nation shifted its attention to the postwar order, Niebuhr's work garnered the attention of the War Department (the precursor to the Department of Defense), which requested permission to translate *The Nature and Destiny of Man* and *The Children of Light and the Children of Darkness* into Japanese to assist in Japanese rebuilding efforts. On the domestic front, Niebuhr helped to found Americans for Democratic Action (ADA), which sought to augment centrist political voices in an era given to ideological extremes. In collaboration with other ADA members such as Eleanor Roosevelt and future vice president Hubert Humphrey, Niebuhr helped launch the "vital center" liberalism that anchored American identity as the nation grew into its new role as a superpower.

Through his writings and activities in this period, Niebuhr influenced leading lights in American life and thought, including political theorists, holders of political office, and public intellectuals across the political spectrum. Among Niebuhr's admirers were Henry Luce, the media mogul who owned *Time* magazine, and Whittaker Chambers, the magazine's senior editor. They decided that Niebuhr's message was vital enough to warrant the platform that the twenty-fifth anniversary edition of *Time* provided. In their judgment, Niebuhr had proven his ability to translate theological hope into political terms that would resonate with *Time*'s readership. With that they gave Niebuhr's message of how to lay hold of hope in bleak times a megaphone.

The Rise of Christian Realism

If the 1930s were the decade in which Niebuhr cultivated a comprehensive theology, the 1940s were marked by his return to politics. This is when he began to operate as a "philosophically inclined, theologically trained political scientist," as his daughter Elisabeth describes it. In addition to his work with the ADA, he helped craft the Roosevelt administration's Four Freedoms declaration and cofounded the Christian Committee on Palestine. His writings strengthened the foundations of postwar democratic theory, and supplied key elements of the conceptual framework for the realist school of international relations that dominated the era's foreign policy. He weighed in on the implications of the atomic bomb, advocated on behalf of the formation of the state of Israel, and consulted for the State Department's Policy Planning Staff. He also traveled extensively, going on State Department-funded trips to England in 1943 and to Germany in 1946. In 1948 he made his way to Amsterdam to attend the first worldwide gathering of Christian leaders following the war, challenging participants to engage the political realm more rigorously and thoughtfully as the fragile postwar order took shape. Underpinning all this activity was the theologically informed political outlook of Christian realism.

Realism has a variety of meanings in political contexts. In a narrower sense the term "realist" is often used as a synonym for practical, pragmatic, or hardheaded. In a broader sense, it describes a comprehensive understanding of how the political realm operates. It is this broader sense that interests us here.[1]

Realist approaches share the view that certain features of human nature—particularly the tendency to act out of self-interest—are constantly at play in political affairs. Yet there is considerable variation in how different forms of realism gauge self-interest and the degree to which it shapes political thought and action. The two variants relevant to the present discussion are theological realism, as exemplified by Christian realism, and what Niebuhr called a "too consistent political realism"[2]—what we might refer to as ultrarealism. Scholar David Halberstam coined the term "ultrarealism" to describe the approach to world politics that came into vogue under the Kennedy administration and shaped US foreign policy through the end of the Vietnam War. Historian Peter Beinart observes that the ultrarealists "started with the reasonable insight that evil would never be eradicated and that the currency of world affairs would always be power—and forgot that there are limits to these truths as well."[3]

Ultrarealism presumes that self-interest is the chief criterion that

1. For a useful overview of different forms of realism, see Robin W. Lovin, *Christian Realism and the New Realism and the New Realities* (New York: Cambridge University Press, 2008), 19-42.

2. Elisabeth Sifton, ed., *Reinhold Niebuhr: Major Works on Religion and Politics* (New York: Library of America, 2015), 317.

3. Peter Beinart, *The Icarus Syndrome: A History of American Hubris* (New York: HarperCollins, 2010), 139.

should shape political behavior. When nations decide whether to sign treaties, form alliances, or make war, they should take the most self-interested course of action. Christian realists agree that self-interest is an overwhelmingly powerful determinant of human behavior, but they do not think this implies that self-interest *should* dictate our political decision making. While considerations of self-interest supply a valuable starting point for political analysis, final decisions should take into account certain ideals of love and justice. Consequently, the Christian realist approach to political issues often differs substantially from the ultrarealist approach.

Ultrarealism understands self-interest in terms of the pursuit of power. It maintains that we make the best political decisions when we presuppose that nations perpetually seek to accumulate power relative to one another. When all political actors operate by this logic, they form treaties and alliances that eventually introduce stability into the political arena by achieving a balance of power. Christian realism, on the other hand, understands self-interest in light of sin's effects on human nature. For the Christian realist, the overwhelming tendency among human beings to act in their perceived self-interest is *one* but not the *only* effect of sin. Sin also distorts how human beings perceive themselves in relation to others. This introduces a gap between what people *perceive* to be in their interest and what is *actually* in their interest, thereby hampering their ability to gauge self-interest accurately. Human beings are driven by self-interest, but are bad at determining what their self-interest is.

The gap between perception and reality accounts in part for why so much of human behavior contains an element of self-sabotage. We see this in the skewed logic of addicts who time and again convince themselves that getting the next fix is the best thing for them. This same gap manifests in politics: from the Carthaginian general Hannibal's failed attempt to conquer Rome to Napoleon's ill-fated invasion of Russia, history brims with examples of how even the shrewdest political strategists prove unable to reconcile their perception of self-interest with political reality.

Christian realism and ultrarealism both presume that self-interest supplies the right starting point for political analysis. Sensitivity to self-interest helps us to perceive dysfunctional dynamics that we might otherwise overlook, and trains us to limit our political expectations to what can realistically be achieved. Both variants of realism also agree that the failure to recognize the central role that self-interest plays in politics can have catastrophic consequences, as Neville Chamberlain's claim to have achieved "peace for our time" following the 1938 Munich Agreement with Hitler attests.

However, unlike ultrarealists, Christian realists do not believe that self-interest is an end in itself. If we consistently seek to serve only our interest, Christian realists argue, our faulty perceptions will cause us to spiral into ever-deeper political dysfunction. Only by aiming for the ideals of love and justice can we begin to address the problems that the distance between perception and reality introduces into our political life. As Robin Lovin puts it, "We have to have trust in a judgment that lies beyond our own judgment. We have to have hope beyond the results of our actions that we can see, and finally we have to have love that keeps us from just being locked into our own self-interest. Those things taken by themselves won't give you a political program, but without faith, hope, and love, you'll never have the motivation and the broad understanding of the human situation to invest your life in changing realities for the people who share this society with you."

In sum, both variants of realism agree on the diagnostic importance of self-interest: taking self-interest seriously is crucial to gauging the stakes of a political situation in a clear-eyed way. Yet the two species of realism disagree as to the role that self-interest should play in the practice of politics. Ultrarealism maintains that self-interest alone is sufficient to achieve a political balance of power, while Christian realists argue that self-interest is not nearly as reliable a criterion as political realists make it out to be. In contrast to ultrarealism, Christian realism asserts that we most effectively mitigate the destructive element in our politics, not through the relentless pursuit of self-interest, but by moving beyond self-interest through pursuing the theologically rich ideals of faith, hope, and love.

While Christian realism is not confined to Niebuhr, he was its chief architect. From *Moral Man and Immoral Society* onward, a keen awareness of self-interest pervades Niebuhr's thought. However, only after the extensive theological engagement of the 1930s did he begin to develop his thinking on the limitations of politics driven by self-interest and the crucial role of ethical ideals in moving us beyond these limitations. Not until *The Children of Light and the Children of Darkness* in 1944 did Niebuhr spell out the Christian realist approach to politics in a comprehensive way. To place this work in context, we return to the period just prior to the December 1941 attack on Pearl Harbor, when Niebuhr responded to a request to participate in one of President Roosevelt's trademark initiatives.

Christian Realism in Action

Niebuhr's increasingly vocal support for the Allied cause garnered the attention of Washington. President Roosevelt had been quietly preparing for US entry into the war. As part of this preparation, the Office of War Information assembled a pamphlet on the four freedoms: freedom of speech, freedom of religion, freedom from want, and freedom from fear. According to Roosevelt, who had introduced them in his January 1941 State of the Union address, all of humanity was entitled to these freedoms. The Four Freedoms campaign was a way of framing the US and Allied war effort as a defense of human rights. Niebuhr was tapped to write the section on the freedom of religion.

Although famed essayist E. B. White edited the pamphlet, the "Freedom of Religion" portion retained a distinctly Niebuhrian flare. "The democratic guarantee of freedom of religion," he wrote, "is not in the nature of a grant—it is in the nature of an admission. It is the state admitting that the spirit soars in illimitable regions beyond the collector of customs."[4] The democratic structure of American government made possible the "miracle" of social cohesion in a religiously pluralistic context. Thus we had the "impressive spectacle . . . of men attending many different churches, but the same town meeting, the same political forum." This contrasted with fascist movements, which "pretend that they own all of man, including his conscience." Denying freedom of worship produced a "political religion in which the leader of the state becomes, himself, the object of worship," and the individual a "corpuscle in the blood of the community, almost without identity."[5] Although the United States had yet to declare war, Niebuhr was already anticipating the rhetorical links among democracy, religion, and freedom that would frame American intervention in world affairs for the remainder of the twentieth century. He would become a vocal critic of the way these terms were deployed after the war, when the United States attained superpower status and began to exert its newfound power throughout the globe. But even before the bombing of Pearl Harbor, Niebuhr was forging the crucial connections between religion and democracy that would undergird the postwar ideological order.

4. E. B. White, ed., *The United Nations Fight for the Four Freedoms* (Washington, DC: Government Printing Office, 1942), 8.

5. White, *Four Freedoms*, 8.

Niebuhr's activism in this period proved similarly prescient. In 1941 he helped found the Union for Democratic Action (UDA), which would evolve into Americans for Democratic Action (ADA) following the war. The initial purpose of the UDA was to provide an outlet for interventionist-minded political activism. As a realist, Niebuhr was aware that effecting change required forming groups that were capable of strategically wielding political leverage. Elisabeth Sifton points out that, when her father first arrived in New York City in the late 1920s, he joined the Socialist Party to help shift the center of political power away from the notoriously corrupt Tammany Hall machine, the entrenched system of patronage that dominated New York politics at the time. But political circumstances had changed drastically over the course of a decade: in 1940, he resigned from the Socialist Party out of protest against its neutral stance toward the war.

This move toward interventionism was the product of Niebuhr's keen appreciation for the tragic character of human life in a sin-ridden world. For Niebuhr this tragic element forced people to choose the lesser of two evils, and in some circumstances the lesser evil could involve the use of violence. While Niebuhr had remained provisionally committed to nonviolence well into the 1930s, theologian Stanley Hauerwas notes, "For Niebuhr the non-violence didn't go all the way down. It was a strategic political move that could achieve certain ends that otherwise might not be achievable in certain circumstances." The rise of fascism in general and the Nazi persecution of the Jews in particular pushed Niebuhr to support entering the fray. Noting that even famed pacifist Dietrich Bonhoeffer participated in an attempt to assassinate Hitler, Sifton observes, "I don't think my father would think . . . that it was ever a good idea to absolutely insist on your initial position and never reconsider it. You have to reconsider it—life makes you reconsider it."

Once the United States entered the war, the debate over interventionism became irrelevant. Niebuhr wasted no time in finding new directions in which to channel his intellectual energies, as a February 1942 article entitled "Jews after the War" demonstrated. This piece was striking both in its grasp of the calamity confronting the Jewish people and in the confidence of Allied victory that fueled its reflections. Only in anticipation of Nazi defeat, after all, could one conceive of postwar circumstances in which the concerns of the Jewish community would play a central role. Following the article's publication, Niebuhr received hundreds of requests to speak to Jewish organizations. Part of this popularity was due to the content of the argument itself. Niebuhr understood the pervasive character of anti-Semitism—which "Hitler did not create but only aggravated"—and the need to take decisive action to confront it.[6] Yet Niebuhr's high demand as a speaker was also indicative of how rare it was for a public figure of his stature to advocate on behalf of the Jews. As scholar Franklin Littell observed, "he was the leading—and at some points the sole—American theologian to understand the crisis posed by Nazism and to intervene on behalf of the survival of the Jewish people."[7]

Niebuhr had first cultivated relationships with Jewish leaders during his time on the Interracial Committee in Detroit. He spoke warmly of his collaboration with Fred Butzel, a Jewish lawyer whose ethical sensibilities he admired. Following his work with Butzel, Niebuhr's account of Judaism began to exhibit a nuance that went well beyond the standard Protestant clichés.[8] Once Hitler had come to power in 1933, Niebuhr expressed alarm over how his anti-Semitic rhetoric could endanger the Jewish population of Germany. By the end of the decade, he was among the community's most vocal Christian supporters. In fact, he was quite blunt about how deep anti-Semitic currents continued to run in Christianity, noting how church attendance in Germany actually increased with the Nazi rise to power.[9]

In light of American Jewry's drastic change in fortunes in the latter half of the twentieth century, it is easy to overlook the extent to which anti-Semitism shaped American attitudes in the lead-up to the war. Once again, the Roosevelt administration's refusal to allow the over nine hundred European Jewish refugees onboard the *St. Louis* to disembark in Miami in May 1939 offers a case in point. By the late 1930s the American populace was well aware of how dire the circumstances for Jews was becoming under Nazi rule. Yet government officials apparently feared that taking in Jewish refugees over and above the immigration quotas set by Congress would stoke anti-immigrant, anti-Semitic sentiment, which in turn would fuel isolationism. These concerns were not unfounded: 83 percent of respondents to a *Fortune* magazine poll opposed easing immi-

6. Sifton, *Reinhold Niebuhr: Major Works*, 640.

7. Franklin Littell, "Reinhold Niebuhr and the Jewish People," *Holocaust and Genocide Studies*, no. 6 (January 1991): 45.

8. Richard Wightman Fox, *Reinhold Niebuhr: A Biography* (Ithaca, NY: Cornell University Press, 1996), 92–93.

9. Egal Feldman, "Reinhold Niebuhr and the Jews," *Jewish Social Studies* 46 (March 4, 1984): 295.

gration restrictions. The *St. Louis* sailed back to Europe, where a quarter of those onboard died in the Holocaust.[10]

It is little wonder then that Niebuhr's article garnered such enthusiastic reception among the Jewish community. In Niebuhr they found a non-Jewish religious leader who not only publicly advocated on their behalf, but also possessed the visibility to draw attention to their plight and to change the minds of his countrymen. This was one of several instances in which Niebuhr took a position that was unpopular at the time but eventually gained mainstream acceptance.

Even in wartime Niebuhr refused to confine his political activity to the relative safety of domestic politics. In the summer of 1943, Niebuhr traveled to England at the invitation of William Temple, the archbishop of Canterbury. On a ten-week tour he spoke to both British audiences and Allied troops, and reported back on the progress of the war.[11] His tidings continued to sound a hopeful tone as he registered his admiration for British resilience in the face of physical and existential threats of war. Yet, in a twist that no doubt took his stateside audience by surprise, he also encouraged his readers to have some sympathy for the foe. Niebuhr asked his readers to put themselves in the shoes of innocent Germans on the ground. Given that "four to ten times as many bombs are raining on the Ruhr region" of Germany as were being dropped on Britain, he wrote, "one is able to envisage the terrible destruction that is being wrought in Germany." Forcing ourselves to confront the carnage of war in this way helps us grasp that "it is not possible to move in history without becoming tainted in guilt."[12] This guilt inflicted spiritual damage that we could only address through a process of confession.

The logic of Niebuhr's argument dovetailed with his appreciation for the pervasiveness of sin. As moral beings, Niebuhr believed, we have an obligation to discern and confess the sins in which we are implicated in our pursuit of even the noblest aims and thereby acknowledge our need for forgiveness. Confession of sin thus becomes a catalyst for cultivating an awareness of how we need the same redemption as our enemies. Historian Andrew Finstuen notes that, in Niebuhr's hands, the notion of

---

10. "Voyage of the *St. Louis*," Holocaust Encyclopedia, last updated July 2, 2016, https://www.ushmm.org/wlc/en/article.php?ModuleId=10005267.

11. Fox, *Reinhold Niebuhr: A Biography*, 216.

12. Reinhold Niebuhr, "The Bombing of Germany," in Sifton, *Reinhold Niebuhr: Major Works*, 654.

original sin is a "leveling doctrine. It's a democratizing doctrine. If all of us are flawed, if all of us fall short of one another and most importantly fall short of the glory of God, then we have a base line to start from." Once we acknowledge that we share the need for forgiveness with even our bitterest enemies, we are free to be more honest about ourselves in general. The notion of original sin thus becomes the "great interpreter of history and politics and [uncovers] the levels of deceit and dishonesty that we have both in our individual lives and in our social and political systems," as Finstuen observes.

The Children of Light and the Children of Darkness

Man's capacity for justice makes democracy possible; man's inclination to injustice makes democracy necessary.
— *The Children of Light and the Children of Darkness*

In January of 1944 Niebuhr brought his Christian realist outlook to the Pacific Coast when he delivered the West Lectures at Stanford. The lectures furnished the material for *The Children of Light and the Children of Darkness*, which was published later that year. Robin Lovin describes this book as an "analysis of the political realities that are at work in the global conflict at that time." It was indeed a timely work that helped shift attention from the conflict itself to key questions about the identity and role of the United States in the postwar era. In an age dominated by collectivist, totalitarian forms of government, Niebuhr offered what he called a "vindication of democracy" on the basis of its ability to accommodate the possibilities and limits of human nature. As Healan Gaston observes, for Niebuhr "the entire democratic project revolves around a Christian view of human nature." This book comprises the most comprehensive example of Niebuhr's Christian realism at work, as it unpacks the political implications of the view of human nature set forth in *The Nature and Destiny of Man*.

At first glance, the title *The Children of Light and the Children of Darkness* appears to reflect the mood of the era. In the midst of World War II, it was all too easy to feel as if the world was divided into spheres of light and darkness as America and the Allies fervently willed the "children of light" to victory. A short way into the book, however, Niebuhr unsettled this stark moral contrast. He drew inspiration for the title from one of Je-

sus's most confounding parables. In the Gospel of Luke, Jesus tells a story
in which a manager who had just been fired by his boss cuts backdoor
deals with his boss's debtors to reduce what they owed. The manager's
motives for these deals are doubly self-serving: he is getting back at his
boss for firing him, and he is doing the debtors a favor so that they would
feel obligated to help him out. In an unexpected twist, when the boss
finds out about what his dishonest manager has done, he does not get
angry. Instead, he commends the manager for behaving shrewdly. Jesus
concludes with the enigmatic observation that "the children of this world
are in their generation wiser than the children of light" (Luke 16:8 KJV).

Citing this passage, Niebuhr identified the children of darkness with
the children of this world. Niebuhr depicted the wisdom of the children of
darkness in political realist terms. He argued that although the children
of darkness "know no law beyond their own will and interest," they have
proven wise, for they "understand the power of self-interest." Through
their "shrewd assessment of the power of self-interest, individual and
national, among the children of light," they have brought the world order to the brink of collapse. The children of light, by contrast, have been
foolish, for they have underestimated the power of self-interest in their
opponents and themselves alike. To overcome the forces of darkness
and establish a workable world order following the war, the children of
light must "appropriate the wisdom of the children of darkness while
remaining free of their malice."[13] They must, in other words, be able to
recognize the good in their enemies and learn from it: a counterintuitive
argument indeed in the midst of such terrible conflict.

The deftness with which Niebuhr elicits, upsets, and reconfigures
the reader's preconceptions attests to his skill as a preacher. In a church
context, ministers must frequently prepare sermons on biblical passages
and stories that their congregations know well. To extract new meaning
from these passages, the minister must figure out how to present the familiar in a different light. Listeners become receptive to new layers of
meaning once they are convinced that there's more to the passage than
they originally thought. Because of his considerable pulpit experience,
Niebuhr knew how to gauge the expectations of his audience. He was
aware of how people would reflexively respond to imagery of light and

---

13. Reinhold Niebuhr, "The Children of Light and the Children of Darkness," in
Sifton, *Reinhold Niebuhr: Major Works*, 362. Hereafter, page references from this work
will be given in parentheses in the text.

darkness in a wartime context, and he strategically leveraged this instinctive reaction to prompt his readers to see both themselves and the emerging world order in a new way.

To make sense of his reconfigured use of light-and-darkness imagery, we must understand the presuppositions that drove his analysis. For Niebuhr the categories of children of light and children of darkness are asymmetrical. Only the most hardened and cynical among us deny the moral obligations to our fellows with enough consistency to qualify as children of darkness. Thus, the vast bulk of humanity belongs to the children of light. The categories, therefore, cannot map neatly on the two sides of the war. Even the ranks of enemy forces are mostly made up of foolish children of light who have been manipulated into channeling their moral impulses to serve the interests of children of darkness.

What the imagery *does* help us grasp is the danger of failing to take self-interest into consideration. To effectively rein in self-interest, the children of light must correctly assess its power and extent. Since they did not grasp the *power* of self-interest, the children of light failed to understand the sheer danger that the cynical children of darkness posed to the world. Since they did not fathom the *extent* to which self-interest operated in every human being, the children of light failed to understand their own vulnerability to manipulation by the children of darkness. Consequently, the children of darkness were able to redirect the moral impulses of foolish children of light toward tyrannical and murderous ends long before other children of light mustered the will to oppose them.

This emphasis on gauging the power and extent of self-interest brings us back to Niebuhr's account of human nature. Much of it by now is familiar: humanity is both finite and free, beset by both good and evil tendencies. Yet here Niebuhr emphasizes the political character of human identity in a way that he has not in previous works. The human being is "by nature social" and thus "cannot fulfill his life within himself but only in responsible and mutual relations with his fellows" (368). He continues, "Man is the kind of animal who cannot merely live. If he lives at all he is bound to seek the realization of his true nature; and to his true nature belongs his fulfillment in the lives of others" (366). This search for "fulfillment in the lives of others" is ultimately what drives politics. Yet this search is complicated by the fact that human beings bring their evil as well as their good impulses into the political arena with them. When acting on their good impulses—that is, in accord with their true nature—human beings strive for harmony with others, for the good always involves the "harmony of the whole [community] on its various levels" (361). However, since they are subject to the effects of original sin, human beings are perennially tempted to short-circuit this process by asserting "some self-interest without regard to the whole" (361). Evil, then, is the product of attempting to achieve fulfillment on one's own terms. Nazism offers an especially vivid portrait of the sheer ruthlessness with which human collectives can assert their interests without any consideration for others. Yet every human collective manifests this tendency to disregard the broader community in the pursuits of its own interests. As Andrew Finstuen observes, "Sin is a bias. It is inherent within us. It is a state of being. It is constitutional. We can do no other but sin even if we can do things that are positive and virtuous."

For Niebuhr, the genius of democracy was that it accommodated the human need for both individual freedom and communal order by starting with a robust appreciation for the power of self-interest. The notion of checks and balances presumed that the various communities that make up a complex society attempt to advance their self-interest. When properly calibrated, these checks and balances set these interests off against each other in a way that results in a "tolerable harmony of the whole" (395). While the results of this system are imperfect, it balances freedom and order more adeptly—and thus results in a greater degree of justice—than political systems that neglect to take adequate stock of self-interest. As a "method for finding proximate solutions to insoluble problems," democracy provides us with the best framework we currently have for building workable societies in a sinful world (420).

Democratic theory contains lessons for relations between nations as well as relations between individuals. Through the shrewd implementation of checks and balances, Niebuhr argued, democracies learn to "beguile, deflect, harness and restrain self-interest, individual and collective, for the sake of the community" (378). But the international community in 1944 had no similar system to restrain self-interest. The customs, mores, and precedents necessary to building an international community capable of channeling self-interest for the good of the whole would develop gradually and tenuously, and would always be vulnerable to being undermined by rogue actors. This prompted Niebuhr to observe that the project of repairing and rebuilding the international order would be the "perpetual problem as well as constant fulfillment of human hopes" (457). The inevitable setbacks on the road to building world community required us to set our hopes higher: "The hope of the

Christian faith that the divine power which bears history can complete, and can purify the corruptions which appear in even the purest human aspirations, is an indispensable prerequisite for the fulfillment of our historic tasks. Without it we are driven to alternate moods of sentimentality and despair; trusting human powers too much in one moment and losing all faith in the meaning of life when we discover the limits of human possibilities" (458).

As toxic as despair can be in our individual lives, when nations behave out of despair the results are catastrophic. To break the vicious cycle of sentimentality and despair, we must approach the task of achieving world community "from the standpoint of a faith which understands the fragmentary and broken character of all historic achievements and yet has confidence in the hands of a Divine Power, whose resources are greater than those of men, and whose suffering love can overcome the corruption of man's achievements, without negating the significance of our striving" (458).

In its final analysis, *The Children of Light and the Children of Darkness* offered a ringing endorsement of democracy chastened by the notion of original sin. Democracy constituted the best available method for recognizing and managing self-interest in the political realm, but only God could enable humans to transcend self-interest, however halting and imperfect that transcendence might be.

Before the fog of war had lifted, Niebuhr was anticipating the need to inject fresh thinking into how we organized our politics. And the key to this fresh thinking could be found in some of the oldest teachings in Christianity. Key shapers of the postwar order took notice of this project. Niebuhr's Christian realism would touch down squarely in the political realm.

The Nuclear Bomb

On May 8, 1945, the long-anticipated defeat of Germany became official. War continued in the Pacific until August of 1945, when the United States dropped nuclear warheads with the incongruous names of Little Boy and Fat Man on the Japanese cities of Hiroshima and Nagasaki. As people started to recognize the awful destructive capacity of the bombs and grasp the implications of living in a nuclearized world, opinions about the US course of action became bitterly polarized. Those who supported the bombings pointed out that they ended what could have been a protracted conflict with high casualties for Allied troops. Those who opposed them argued that it was impossible to justify the use of technology that leveled cities and took hundreds of thousands of lives with a single detonation.

By the fall of 1945, Niebuhr was already offering his characteristically ambivalent commentary on the issue. In an article entitled "The Atomic Bomb," Niebuhr did not mince words in describing the moral implications of the bomb's use: "Critics have rightly pointed out that we reached the level of Nazi morality in justifying the use of the bomb on the grounds that it shortened the war," thereby proving that "total war was not a Nazi invention."[14] He also singled out those implicated in the decision to use the bomb for their "lack of imagination in impressing the enemy with the use of the bomb without the wholesale loss of life that attended our demonstration of its power."[15] Niebuhr seemed to be suggesting that a nuclear test in full view of Japanese leaders might have convinced them to surrender. Yet, as a realist, he did not think it was possible to prevent further development of the technology or to confine nuclear technology to civilian rather than military uses. Imposing restraints on nuclear technology would require a level of cooperation between nations that could take decades to develop. Meanwhile, Niebuhr believed, we had little choice but to learn to accommodate our politics to the realities of a nuclear world. In later work reflecting on the prospect of the hydrogen bomb, Niebuhr would point out that the sheer destructive power of nuclear technology may prevent its use: "If we had to use this kind of destruction to save our lives, would we find life worth living?"[16] Robin Lovin observes that as Niebuhr built on these insights, he would become "one of the first thinkers to really understand the logic of deterrence, namely, that you have to be prepared to threaten to use these weapons in order to ensure that they will not be used."

Niebuhr's position did not satisfy either side of the nuclear debate. From the standpoint of nuclear critics, despite his condemnation of the bomb Niebuhr provided little ethical basis for countering the spread of nuclear weapons. Niebuhr criticized those who deployed nuclear weap-

---

14. Reinhold Niebuhr, "The Atomic Bomb," in *Love and Justice: Selections from the Shorter Writings of Reinhold Niebuhr*, ed. D. B. Robertson (Philadelphia: Westminster, 1957), 233.

15. Niebuhr, "The Atomic Bomb," 233.

16. Reinhold Niebuhr, "The Hydrogen Bomb," in Robertson, *Love and Justice*, 237.

onry for their lack of imagination, and in a nuclear world, moral imagination was more needed than ever. Where was the evidence of such imagination at work in Niebuhr's own view? Meanwhile, from the standpoint of nuclear apologists, Niebuhr's condemnation was too forceful. Was it really worth risking a protracted conflict that could have resulted in a similar total loss of life? Furthermore, life in a nuclear world required greater resolve, not less. Why risk undermining this resolve through scathing self-criticism?

The nuclear bomb provides a useful illustration of Niebuhr's Christian realist logic at work. As a Christian ethicist, he did not shy away from making moral judgments: by deploying the bomb, "we sinned grievously against the law of God and against the people of Japan," he wrote in 1946.[17] Yet, as a realist, he was committed to beginning his moral reflection by taking an unflinching look at the political situation as it stood. Rather than dwelling on how things should be, he sought to nudge present political circumstances in the most morally responsible direction; hence, he both condemned the bombings and saw the practical value of deterrence.

Christian realism is designed to cultivate an uneasy conscience. Highlighting both the moral stakes and the moral ambiguities of a given issue staves off the self-righteousness of artificial moral clarity on the one hand and the cynicism of *Realpolitik* on the other. Whatever else might be said of Niebuhr's approach, one thing is clear: he would not let his audience settle for pat answers to thorny moral questions.

The State of Israel

In 1946 Niebuhr turned his attention back to advocating on behalf of the Jewish community. As the atrocities of the Nazi regime came to light, the push to establish a new state of Israel in Palestine, also known as Zionism, took on new urgency. Yet the issue of a Jewish state remained fraught with controversy. On one side of the debate, certain sectors of the Jewish community were resistant to the notion of a secular Jewish state. Others against the notion argued that the establishment of the state of Israel would require the unjust confiscation of Palestinian land. On the other hand, anti-Semitism continued to be a powerful force in the

17. Fox, *Reinhold Niebuhr: A Biography*, 224.

years immediately following the war. A Gallup poll in 1945 found that a quarter of prospective voters would support an anti-Jewish candidate for Congress.[18] Faced with both the Nazi attempt to eliminate them from the face of the earth and the ongoing reality of anti-Semitism, many within the Jewish community felt that their very survival as a people depended on the success of the Zionist movement.

It was in this environment that Reinhold Niebuhr arrived—uninvited—to testify at the Anglo-American Committee of Inquiry meeting in Washington, DC, in January of 1946. The committee had been appointed to consider whether to permit the immigration of one hundred thousand Jewish persons to Palestine. As an unscheduled speaker, Niebuhr was not guaranteed a hearing. He got the opportunity to deliver his statement only because a speaker slated to protest the Zionist position neglected to show up. His name: Henry Sloane Coffin, the president of Union Seminary and Niebuhr's boss.[19] This shows how deeply divisive the issue was, even among religious leaders who were familiar with the plight of European Jews under Nazi rule.

Following the testimony, Rabbi Stephen Wise wrote Niebuhr an appreciative letter, noting that the lead lawyer for the Zionist contingent called his testimony the "finest presentation of the Zionist case that I have ever heard." Niebuhr had "showed why the Jewish state in Palestine was a necessity, not just for the Displaced Jews of Europe but for all Jews."[20] While it is not possible to gauge precisely how Niebuhr's statement affected the deliberations, the committee did end up recommending that the immigration be permitted. The decision to admit the refugees helped lay the groundwork for the formation of the state of Israel in 1948.

From our standpoint seventy years after Israel was founded, the politics surrounding the state of Israel have hardly grown less controversial. We do not know how Niebuhr would have responded to the Yom Kippur War, the Palestinian refugee crisis, or the intifadas. But we do know the historical context in which he voiced such staunch support. Jewish Studies professor Susannah Heschel observes, "Niebuhr seems to have been very, very aware that after the end of World War II and with the murder

18. Harold E. Quinley and Charles Y. Glock, *Antisemitism in America* (New Brunswick, NJ: Transaction Books, 1983), 17.

19. Fox, *Reinhold Niebuhr: A Biography*, 226.

20. Niebuhr Papers, Library of Congress.

of 6 million Jews and the thousands and thousands of Jewish refugees who were being held in displaced persons camps all over Europe, the effort to create a state out of the Jewish homeland . . . had to happen."[21]

Niebuhr was also mindful of the anti-Semitism in his own backyard. *New York Times* columnist David Brooks notes that Niebuhr "saw anti-Semitism firsthand" when he had opposed the Ku Klux Klan in Detroit. This helped instill in him an appreciation for the fact that "groups can get clannish, can get tribal, can get oppressive."[22] He adds, "it would make sense for someone growing out of that [to] want Jews to have sanctuary in the state of Israel."

As much as Niebuhr emphasized the moral ambiguity of human affairs and the need to be self-critical when intervening in history, he took decisive stands when he felt that the situation required him to do so. Even so, Elisabeth Sifton reminds us that Niebuhr "saw this as a partial solution to the terrible difficulties that Jewish people faced after the conclusion of the war." Once again, Niebuhr's Christian realism rejected facile solutions to complex political problems.

The Corridors of Power

By 1947 Niebuhr's influence began to be felt in mainstream politics. Niebuhr dissolved the Union for Democratic Action (UDA) to help form Americans for Democratic Action (ADA), which Elisabeth Sifton describes as a "kind of pressure group to pester the Democratic Party to advance the causes of social justice." Following the war, the domestic political landscape changed drastically. The American economy expanded rapidly to accommodate wartime needs, and by the end of the conflict, the United States had the largest, most robust economy on earth. There was also no longer any question about American involvement in world affairs. Through sheer economic and military power, the United States was the de facto leader of the Western world. In this reconfigured political landscape, the fault lines between liberals and conservatives that held sway prior to the war no longer obtained.

21. Journey Films interview with Susannah Heschel, May 31, 2016. Unless otherwise noted, subsequent quotes attributed to Susannah Heschel are from this interview.

22. Journey Films interview with David Brooks, August 2, 2016. Unless otherwise noted, subsequent quotes attributed to Brooks are from this interview.

Through the ADA Niebuhr joined forces with like-minded centrists and progressives to mobilize an antifascist, anticommunist voice in American politics. Other founding members included Eleanor Roosevelt, future vice president Hubert Humphrey, and Harvard historian Arthur Schlesinger Jr., whose book *The Vital Center* helped to lay the groundwork for the ADA's understanding of liberalism. Schlesinger described this vital center as delineating the midpoint between the totalitarianisms at either extreme of the political spectrum: fascism on the right and communism on the left. To inoculate themselves against these forms of totalitarianism, the nonfascist right and noncommunist left needed to adopt a "democratic faith" grounded in a sober assessment of the limits of human nature.[23]

If this sounds like Niebuhr, it is no coincidence. In his memoirs, Schlesinger discussed how he immersed himself in both *The Children of Light and the Children of Darkness* and *The Nature and Destiny of Man* as he crafted his argument.[24] Part of what made this remarkable was that Schlesinger was a self-described agnostic. Yet he still found Niebuhr's account of human nature compelling, and he showed a Niebuhrian penchant for using religious language to describe political systems. "Vital center" liberalism would be an important influence on American politics for the next two decades. Gary Dorrien observes that Niebuhr personified the vital center "at least as well or better than any other individual." Niebuhr was indeed pivotal to the articulation of the conceptual underpinnings for centrist politics throughout the era.

As active as he was on the domestic front, Niebuhr was arguably an even greater influence on international relations. His realist approach garnered the attention of future CIA director Allen Dulles, who recommended him for membership on the Council of Foreign Relations in 1946. In 1947 the War Department requested (and obtained) permission to translate *The Nature and Destiny of Man* and *The Children of Light and the Children of Darkness* into Japanese for publication and distribution in Japan. In 1948 University of Chicago professor Hans Morgenthau published *Politics among Nations*, which established him as the foremost figure of the realist school of international relations that dominated mid-

---

23. Arthur Schlesinger Jr., *The Vital Center: The Politics of Freedom* (New Brunswick, NJ: Transaction Publishers, 1998), 245.

24. Arthur Schlesinger Jr., *A Life in the Twentieth Century: Innocent Beginnings, 1917–1950* (New York: Houghton Mifflin, 2000), 511–12.

century American foreign policy. He was a close friend of Niebuhr's, and freely credited him as a major influence on his thinking.

Perhaps the clearest indication of the high regard in which influential figures in foreign policy held Niebuhr during this period came in 1949. Niebuhr began consulting for the State Department's Policy Planning Staff at the invitation of George Kennan, the author of the famous "Mr. X" article that helped launch the Cold War policy of containment. As to why Niebuhr was invited to join the council, Elisabeth Sifton points out that Kennan "respected my father's intelligence about complex world affairs." Niebuhr accepted the invitation, as he thought that his theological training gave him a perspective that would "deepen and help the conversation." Niebuhr, in short, was one of the main shapers of both the theory and the practice of international relations in the mid-twentieth century.

Niebuhr's pervasive influence helps explain why he emerged as a candidate to appear on *Time* magazine's twenty-fifth anniversary cover. But Niebuhr had not always seen eye to eye with Time's owner, media mogul Henry Luce. Several months before the bombing of Pearl Harbor, Niebuhr wrote, "Mr. Luce is to be distrusted. . . . He does not show the slightest indication that our salvation can be worked out only in fear and trembling."[25] This goes to show that Henry Ford was far from the only prominent figure that Niebuhr publicly called out. As Robin Lovin observes, "Niebuhr took full advantage of living in a liberal democracy and being able to be offensive to people who were in power." Yet, by decade's end, even those he had offended were beginning to recognize the value of his perspective. Kennan's fabled "long telegram" from Moscow in February of 1946 alerted the State Department to the expansionist ambitions of the Soviet Union. The following month, Winston Churchill's "Iron Curtain" speech at Westminster College in Missouri captured the attention and imagination of the public. As people in positions of power grew convinced that the United States would get roped into a protracted standoff with the Soviet Union, they started to recognize the strategic utility of deploying religious symbolism and vocabulary to frame the conflict. Who better to symbolize the political power of religious language than the man who almost singlehandedly placed the notion of sin squarely within the day's political discourse?

The article on Niebuhr that accompanied the cover image was entitled "Faith for a Lenten Age." It described Niebuhr's thought as "the

25. Fox, *Reinhold Niebuhr: A Biography*, 202.

oldtime religion put through the intellectual ringer."[26] "An intellectual's intellectual," wrote *Time*'s editor, Whittaker Chambers, "he nevertheless lectures and preaches with the angular arm-swinging of a revivalist."[27] And, like a revivalist, he made the notion of sin central to his message. Although the article was intended for a popular audience, Chambers offered a sophisticated take on Niebuhr's view of original sin, the paradoxes of human life, and how religious vocabulary illumines the challenges of politics. This was a cultural moment in which readers were accustomed to having their points of view challenged and their attention spans tested.

Niebuhr's appearance on *Time*'s cover catapulted him into the public eye like never before. It is a major part of why he is commonly remembered — and often derided — as the "establishment theologian." Yet Niebuhr would soon find out that *Time*'s owner, Henry Luce, had set ideas about the role of religion in political discourse. In January 1949, Luce wrote Niebuhr a letter explaining why he had rejected an article Niebuhr had submitted to *Fortune*, another magazine under the aegis of Luce's media empire. "Your article," Luce wrote, "is addressed to a country which, confident or over-confident in its rightness, is taking vigorous initiative in the world. I see, at the moment, no such America." He continued, "If I may use military terms . . . your article is written to a powerful country on the offensive; I think, on the contrary, that we are on the defensive — a country dissipating its power, tragically, on a false and stultifying defensive."[28]

Luce was intent on using his platform to deepen America's resolve rather than interrogate its role in world affairs. How differently indeed the two men construed the relationship of human nature to power! Whereas both agreed on the necessity of wielding power, Niebuhr saw power as inherently threatening to one's moral integrity. To avoid being consumed by it, one needed to approach its use with fear and trembling. For Luce, adopting the right moral platform safeguarded and legitimized one's use of power. By this logic, strengthening the nation's moral resolve would enhance the nation's ability to deploy power correctly. Self-critique, by contrast, could sap this resolve before it adequately developed. David Brooks echoes a similar critique: "Where I fault Niebuhr is that some-

---

26. Whittaker Chambers, "Faith for a Lenten Age," *Time*, March 8, 1948, 71.
27. Chambers, "Faith for a Lenten Age," 76.
28. Reinhold Niebuhr Papers, Library of Congress.

times to motivate people you need a certain trumpet. You need a clarion call, you need to play on their idealism. You need to play on people's romantic sense that we really can change things . . . you won't face off the Soviet Union, you won't try to end world hunger or end AIDS, if you're filled from day one of any project with self-criticism and self-remorse and self-suspicion."

Had Niebuhr replied to Luce, he might have highlighted the strangeness of depicting the country that dropped two nuclear bombs as lacking in resolve. Or questioned how a nation that was actively laying the groundwork for the NATO alliance was "dissipating" its power. Niebuhr might also have pointed out that, when the most powerful nation on the globe regarded words of caution as dangerous attempts to weaken its resolve, the morally corrosive character of power had already done its damage. For Niebuhr, self-critique did not undermine resolve; rather, it tempered it. By bringing the ulterior motives underlying the exercise of power to light, self-critique was instrumental in helping us "beguile, deflect, harness and restrain self-interest . . . for the sake of the community."[29] To dismiss self-critique was to jettison a crucial device for bringing our actions under the scrutiny of a higher law.

Luce closed the letter by stating, "Please do not take my name off the list of your disciples, either personally or professionally." But the overriding point was clear: Niebuhr could leverage his access to Luce's media empire to advance American interests, but not to critique them. It was now evident that Niebuhr's influence came at a price: the powerful would appropriate Niebuhr when it suited their interests, but brush him aside when he challenged them too directly.

Both elements of this dynamic were on display during Yale's search for a new president in 1949. To Niebuhr's surprise, he emerged on the short list of candidates. Fox notes that his "state department duties must have helped legitimate him as a serious candidate: they demonstrated that he was familiar with the corridors of power, with lofty responsibilities."[30] Yet the official offer never materialized. Yale, it seems, was attracted to Niebuhr's prestige, but did not want to assume the risks of putting him at the helm.

29. Sifton, *Reinhold Niebuhr: Major Works*, 378.
30. Fox, *Reinhold Niebuhr: A Biography*, 239.

The Clash of the "Supertheologians"

For much of the 1940s, Niebuhr had devoted his energies to political questions: How should the United States get involved in World War II? What shape will the world order take following the war? How do we craft theories of democracy and international relations to suit this world? In the summer of 1948, however, Niebuhr turned his attention to a religious question: What is the role of Christianity in the postwar context?

The newly formed World Council of Churches held its inaugural conference in Amsterdam during the summer of 1948. The council was formed to promote communication and collaboration among Christian churches and denominations worldwide. The conference's topic, "Man's Disorder and God's Design," suited the tenor of a time in which the future of humanity seemed as tenuous as ever. The conference featured a confrontation between two of the most influential religious thinkers of the twentieth century: Reinhold Niebuhr and the great Swiss-German theologian Karl Barth.

Barth had risen swiftly to worldwide renown in the early 1920s after publishing a revised version of his commentary on the apostle Paul's epistle to the Romans. Like Niebuhr, Barth at first had been committed to the liberal Protestant perspective that emphasized the capacity of humanity to comprehend and enact the will of God. Yet, when German church leaders publicly supported what would become one of history's most brutal and senseless conflicts in World War I, Barth became disillusioned. He came to believe that, by enlisting the prestige of the Almighty to legitimate such horror, German Christianity showcased the extent to which it had allowed a shallow faith in human reason to supplant obedience to God. In response, Barth emphasized the chasm separating God and humanity, and the utter inability of sinful human beings to bridge this chasm using the tools of reason. When human beings attempt to portray God using human categories, Barth argued, they end up with an elaborate projection of themselves. As Barth so memorably put it, "One cannot speak of God simply by speaking of man in a loud voice."[31] In Barth's framework, we can avoid remaking God in our image only by renouncing the temptation to make God intelligible to ourselves and to others.

31. Karl Barth, *The Word of God and the Word of Man* (London: Hodder and Stoughton, 1935), 196.

Instead, we must accept God's revelation by faith and obey it without seeking to make it respectable by human standards.

Niebuhr appreciated Barth's corrective to the liberal project, although he felt that Barth took the critique too far. In his effort to insulate Christianity from human meddling, Barth stripped people of faith of any apparatus for drawing meaningful distinctions between right and wrong in everyday life. While Barth was right to emphasize the distance between a righteous God and sinful humanity, he overlooked the ways in which human beings still retained the ability to comprehend and implement the love and justice revealed in the Bible. Niebuhr conceded freely that this pursuit of justice would require continual repentance and receptivity to divine grace, and even then would be riddled with problems that God alone could overcome. Yet, even so, human beings remained responsible before God and one another to strive for justice. Robin Lovin describes the contrast between the thinkers: "[They] represented really opposing ways of thinking about Christianity and the relationship to democracy and society. Barth, because he was worried about the way that Christianity and Germany had been taken over by the Nazi movement, always wanted to distinguish the church from society. Niebuhr's realism led him to be worried about the way the church was embedded in the life of society and to think about how we could use that for purposes of achieving a greater justice."

This was, in effect, a showdown between two of the great voices of conscience of the era: the American voice of Reinhold Niebuhr and the European voice of Karl Barth. These two thinkers had much in common: both their perspectives had been informed by the turmoil of the early twentieth century, and each had rebelled against what he saw as the fecklessness of religion that placed undue faith in human reason. But while they had each transformed the ethical conversations in his respective sphere of influence, they viewed the role of religious institutions in the postwar era differently.

This debate took on particular urgency in the context of 1948. With the United Nations in its fragile infancy, religious institutions played the vital political function of supplying relatively functional, stable, and proven transnational networks in a world that was only beginning to rebuild after the war. In light of the participation of representatives from a vast swath of global Christianity, the World Council of Churches' conference proceedings would help shape the way these networks would interface with the postwar world.

The contours of the Niebuhr/Barth debate become clear in their respective conference addresses. In his opening statements, Barth asserted: "We ought to give up, even on our first day of deliberations, every thought that the care of the church, the care of the world, is our care. Burdened with this thought we should straighten out nothing; we should only increase disorder in church and world still more. For this is the root of all human disorder: the dreadful, godless, ridiculous opinion that man is the Atlas who is destined to bear the dome of heaven upon his shoulders." For Barth, the work of overcoming the effects of evil had already been accomplished in the death and resurrection of Jesus. The task for Christians was to bear witness to this victory over evil, not to be God's "lawyers, engineers, managers, statisticians and administrative directors" in some sort of "Christian Marshall Plan," as he called it.[32]

Over the course of the conference, there were animated discussions between the Niebuhrian and Barthian camps. In his closing remarks, Niebuhr clearly had Barth's opening statements in mind. "From the standpoint of our Christian faith," Niebuhr noted, "we know that God will be exalted and his mercy and judgment assured though empires and civilizations perish." But, Niebuhr continued, we must not stop there: "We cannot derive from our ultimate faith an irresponsible attitude to this perplexing situation in which we stand. We must work while it is day. And we will work the more diligently if we are not harassed by fears of the perils of the night, since we worship a Lord who is Lord of both day and night, having conquered darkness, night, and death in the Cross and the Resurrection."[33] Christian faith, in other words, supplies the strength to face down the world's evils without despair. And face them Christians must, lest they prove too heavenly minded to be of any earthly good. They must show themselves to be wise children of light.

The difference in Niebuhr's and Barth's respective positions came down to the implications they attached to Jesus's death and resurrection. Both figures saw these events as signaling God's ultimate triumph over evil, but they had different visions of how they shaped present action. For Barth the good news of the Christian message was that this triumph

32. Karl Barth, "No Christian Marshall Plan," *Christian Century*, December 8, 1948, 1330-33.

33. The audio of Niebuhr's World Council of Churches address, as well as several other sermons and lectures, may be found on the website On Being with Krista Tippett: http://www.onbeing.org/program/moral-man-and-immoral-society-rediscovering -reinhold-niebuhr/feature/sermons-and-lectures.

was *already* complete. In light of this, the task of Jesus's followers was to bear witness to the victory that has already been achieved. This witness exposed the futility of evil and helped to open human beings to the healing and transformative work of grace. For Niebuhr the good news of the Christian message was that Jesus's death and resurrection *inaugurated* God's triumph over evil, which would be completed at the final judgment. In the meantime, the task of followers of Jesus was to become participants in the process of God's unfolding work of redemption, finding the strength to face present evils without despair in their hope that history *would be* redeemed.

From their respective standpoints, the other's position seemed crucially flawed. For Barth, the preoccupation of Niebuhr and his ilk with making the gospel relevant was the product of relying too heavily on human ability and judgment, thereby emptying the Christian message of its power. Niebuhr, in other words, was offering another variant of the ineffectual Christianity from which both of them had strived so hard to break free. In Niebuhr's view, Barth's arresting portrait of sin and redemption was spiritually edifying in times of great upheaval, but supplied little guidance over the ethical terrain of everyday life. Barth's approach to ethics could, in Niebuhr's words, "fight the devil if he shows both horns and both cloven feet. But it refuses to make discriminating judgments between good and evil if the devil shows only one horn or the half of a cloven foot."[34]

The conference served to clarify the two thinkers' differences rather than to resolve them. The lines they drew in their debate continue to shape contemporary discussions over issues at the intersection of faith and politics: To what extent should churches weigh in on political issues? How should they leverage their moral authority? Where does this moral authority come from? Are religious institutions supposed to provide a haven from a broken world, or are they supposed to supply a platform for engaging the world? These issues are no less urgent in today's era of religious extremism than they were at the conclusion of World War II. Listen in on these discussions carefully enough, and you will hear echoes of Niebuhr and Barth.

34. Reinhold Niebuhr, "We Are Men and Not God," *Christian Century*, October 27, 1948, 1139.

Facing New Challenges

As the decade drew to a close, the world Niebuhr had envisioned was rapidly materializing. The United Nations was up and running, the state of Israel had become a reality, and with the formation of NATO and implementation of the Marshall Plan to rebuild Western Europe, the United States was taking a leadership role in world affairs that would have been unimaginable a decade earlier. The crisis of confidence in American institutions and democratic forms of governance that characterized the Great Depression era had passed.

Its passing gave Niebuhr something of a paradoxical standing in American life. On the one hand, he enjoyed greater prestige than any other wartime religious leader. He had been proven right on the need for intervention, on the viability of democracy, and on the need for the formation of the Jewish state. When Niebuhr spoke, the corridors of power took note. Supreme Court justices, media moguls, foreign policy experts, and prominent politicians counted themselves among his admirers. And his Christian realism was taken seriously, prompting even ardent secularists to invoke the language of sin when seeking to make sense of politics.

Yet Niebuhr would find himself marginalized in the world that he had helped usher in. In the lead-up to the war, Niebuhr's characteristically somber analysis had been laced with hope: that the Allies would win the war long before its outcome was certain; that democracy would find its footing in a world ravaged by totalitarianism; that nations would figure out how to form a viable world community. It was his ability to point others toward hope in the face of crisis that enabled him to articulate a "faith for a Lenten age," as *Time* magazine put it. Yet, as the United States grew into its role as a superpower, the more somber elements of Niebuhr's message increasingly fell on deaf ears. Leaders in various sectors of American life no longer wanted to hear about the corrosive character of power or be reminded of the moral peril of hubris. They were quick to apply these lessons to other nations, but slow to take a long, hard look at themselves, as Niebuhr had prescribed. They co-opted Niebuhr's prestige without subjecting themselves to his critique.

Niebuhr had stirred the American conscience to venture into the fog of war and face the moral ambiguities of world leadership. And the nation that had been so reluctant to enter the fray was beginning to grow confident in formulas for dealing with the challenges of power — too confident. For the last decade, he had spoken words of hope to stave off despair; now, he would need to find ways to rouse his audience from complacency.

But this new chapter demanded more of Niebuhr than he had left to give. At decade's end, he was fifty-seven years old, and the frenetic pace at which he had lived his life was taking its toll. On multiple occasions throughout the 1940s he had worked himself to exhaustion. In America's time of crisis, he had managed to recover his energies; but as the nation grew prosperous, his health would force him to slow down.

CHAPTER FOUR

Bumbling Knights and Nuclear Warheads

A blinding flash of light streaks across the horizon. As it fades, a cloud in the shape of a mushroom grows impossibly large over a barren stretch of the Nevada desert. This ominous sight is met with applause and the clinking of cocktail glasses. After all, this is Vegas.

For several years beginning in 1951, atomic tests were conducted roughly every three weeks in a remote area sixty-five miles away from the Strip. In other regions of the country, these tests might have been greeted with protest; Vegas's leading lights, however, saw things differently. Local entrepreneurs organized bomb-viewing parties and excursions to prime viewing sites. Area shops stocked all manner of atomic kitsch, from coffee mugs and T-shirts to images of pinup girls sporting stylized mushroom clouds as bathing suits. The world might have trembled before the nuclear bomb, but in Vegas, they commodified it.[1]

The 1950s were a decade of contrasts. On the one hand, never had the United States—or any nation, for that matter—been so wealthy and powerful. The most wild-eyed optimist of a decade earlier could not have imagined the swiftness and scale of the country's turn of fortune. The United States had embraced its role as world leader with aplomb: by 1948 it had set in motion the Marshall Plan, which accelerated the rebuilding of Western Europe and spearheaded the NATO alliance. The isolationism that had dominated American politics prior to the bombing of Pearl Harbor was a distant memory.

---

1. For more, see "Las Vegas: An Unconventional History," part of PBS's *American Experience* series, http://www.pbs.org/wgbh/amex/lasvegas/peopleevents/e_atomic-tourism.html.

On the other hand, the 1950s were filled with profound anxiety. The specter of nuclear war cast a pall over American society, as the schoolchildren who underwent duck-and-cover drills can attest. This shadow was cast in part by the sense that the United States was precariously perched between the chaos of a planet racked by poverty and the tyrannical order represented by the Soviet bloc. Communities across the country fretted over communist infiltration of American society, a fear that gave rise to the "red scare" and McCarthyism.

The dawn of the decade also found the nation in a religious frame of mind. In the early 1950s rates of church attendance skyrocketed; evangelists such as Baptist minister Billy Graham filled stadiums; radio personalities such as Catholic bishop Fulton Sheen reached audiences of millions; and pastor Norman Vincent Peale's classic *The Power of Positive Thinking* besieged the *New York Times* best-seller list for nearly four years.[2]

Yet this was also an era of decadence and complacency. As the austerity of depression and war gave way to an unprecedented economic boom, America morphed into a consumerist society obsessed with attaining ever-higher standards of living. Forms of entertainment that catered to escapist impulses—professional sports, the Hollywood movie industry, and televised game shows—proliferated. And as Americans crusaded for justice overseas, they continued to oppress their fellow citizens at home with Jim Crow laws and other forms of race discrimination.

The Vegas bomb parties captured something of these contradictory impulses at work in the American consciousness: they turned horror into entertainment and profit; they transformed the very act of facing our fears into a means of escape; and they numbed us to the crystal-clear evidence of profound issues in our society and in the world more broadly. In typical fashion, Reinhold Niebuhr sensed the implications of these discrepant forces and searched for a way to articulate them to the American public. He settled on using irony as a lens through which to view the nation's past and make sense of its present role on the world stage. In Niebuhr's hands, irony highlighted the gap between our self-perception as a nation and the realities of the Cold War world. And irony helped us come to terms with our limits in ways that helped us negotiate our place in this world with greater humility, wisdom, and—surprisingly enough—

---

2. Ron Alexander, "Chronicle," *New York Times*, May 31, 1994, http://www.nytimes .com/1994/05/31/nyregion/chronicle-254657.html.

humor. The result was Niebuhr's final masterpiece, *The Irony of American History* (1952), which retired army colonel and military historian Andrew Bacevich calls "the most important book ever written about US foreign policy," with "the greatest enduring value in helping us understand who we are and why we do what we do in the world."[3] As we shall see, irony also supplies an apt motif for understanding Niebuhr's own role in American society in this era.

What to Do with Reinhold Niebuhr?

In 1951 Niebuhr became the subject of an FBI investigation. Bureau employees gathered extensive information about his past, interviewed his former neighbors, and interrogated his wife Ursula. Their daughter Elisabeth even recalls seeing investigators "creeping around the card catalogue" at Union Theological Seminary.

This may seem a strange way to treat the man who had recently been feted on the cover of *Time* as the man of the hour, and who, in the words of Gary Dorrien, would come to be seen as one of the "architects of the Cold War." But such were the paradoxes of American society at midcentury. In a decade, the nation had gone from isolationism to world leadership; from the doldrums of the Great Depression to unprecedented economic prosperity; and from the margins of the world stage to superpower status. Americans struggled to come to terms with this breathtaking rate of change and what it meant.

With great power comes inclination to paranoia. Those who succumb to this temptation become consumed with identifying and neutralizing potential threats to their power. In extreme cases this leads to mass violence, as it did during Stalin's purges. More commonly it takes the form of excessive surveillance and witch hunts, such as occurred under Senator Joseph McCarthy during the "red scare" of the early 1950s.

Americans became aware of their superpower status and of Soviet expansion nearly simultaneously. As the two nations competed for dominance on the world stage, many Americans came to see the conflict in ideological terms: America was God-fearing, while Soviet communism was godless; Americans were a free people, while communists were cogs

---

3. Journey Films interview with Andrew Bacevich, April 12, 2016. Unless otherwise noted, subsequent quotes attributed to Bacevich are from this interview.

in a totalitarian machine. With this ideological dichotomy in mind, Americans began to fear infiltration: ideologies, after all, are no respecters of borders. If the distinctions between American democracy and Soviet communism boiled down to a set of beliefs, then the conflict between them was ultimately over hearts and minds. Communist ways of thinking could take root in one's countrymen at any moment, and the most effective way to prevent ideology from taking hold was through perpetual hypervigilance.

The appeal to this approach was that it offered clarity and safety: it promised to identify and uproot the dangerous element in American society before it could threaten the American way of life. Yet it proved incapable of accommodating nuance. It presupposed that people could be sorted into one of two camps: God-fearing, freedom-loving patriots, or godless enemies of freedom. But *can* we divide humanity along such stark black-and-white categories? What about people who profess belief in God but don't go to church, or churchgoers who struggle with doubt? Does either fit squarely in the "godly" camp? What about war heroes who happen to be agnostic — does their lack of religion negate their patriotism? Or people of faith who oppose the American way on religious grounds — do their criticisms of country invalidate their status as "godly"?

And what to do with a figure like Reinhold Niebuhr — a former socialist-turned-Cold War adviser, a man of the cloth who counted atheists among his most vocal admirers and friends? How does one categorize a figure who penned both the eloquent defense of democracy in *The Children of Light and the Children of Darkness* and the scathing, Marxist-influenced critiques of *Moral Man and Immoral Society*?

The FBI file on Niebuhr would end up over six hundred pages long. Investigators seemed to believe that tracking down one more article or interviewing one more acquaintance would supply that missing piece that would solve the riddle of Reinhold Niebuhr. But Niebuhr's life and thought defied neat categorization. He both shaped and subverted American identity in such basic ways that any attempt to label him as *either* a formative *or* a disruptive influence was futile.

It is little wonder that Niebuhr gravitated toward the concept of irony as he wrote one of his most influential books. Not only was it apt for describing the American situation; it also helped make sense of his own life as someone who was both consulting for the State Department and being investigated by the FBI.

The Irony of American History

The final wisdom of life requires, not the annulment of incongruity but the achievement of serenity within and above it.

— *The Irony of American History*

The early 1950s marked a turn in Niebuhr's thinking from politics to history. Much had changed since Niebuhr had taken his first pastorate: he had moved from Detroit to New York, from the pastorate to the professorate, and from obscurity to national fame. And the world in which he now lived was similarly unrecognizable — it had been transformed by economic booms and crises, a massive world war, the advent of nuclear power, and realignment into communist and anticommunist blocs. Niebuhr had previously focused on addressing each of these issues as it arose. Now he wanted to link them, to reflect on how to interpret the arc of history.

Niebuhr was not merely concerned with the historian's task of making sense of the ebb and flow of human events; he sought to articulate how humanity's relationship to God shaped the way that we think and talk about history. If America, in all its awesome power, was accountable to a God before whom "the nations are as a drop in the bucket and are counted as small dust in the balances" (Isa. 40:15)[4] — how would this inform the way we saw ourselves as a nation? How would it shape our actions and policies relative to other nations? How would it put our role as historical actors into perspective?

This theological approach to history enabled Niebuhr to bring together the various elements of his big-picture thinking: the political realm of human interaction, the spiritual realm of the individual's relationship to God, and the God's-eye view of human events. *The Irony of American History* showcases Niebuhr's thinking at its broadest, which is why this is arguably the most widely influential of his books. Political scientists, historians, scholars of religion, specialists in American studies, and an array of public figures from activists to presidents have attested to the ways that *Irony* has shaped their life and thought.

In 1630, before disembarking in the New World, John Winthrop, Pu-

---

4. Reinhold Niebuhr, "The Irony of American History," in *Reinhold Niebuhr: Major Works on Religion and Politics*, ed. Elisabeth Sifton (New York: Library of America, 2015), 572. Hereafter, page references from this work will be given in parentheses in the text.

ritan minister and governor of the Massachusetts Bay Colony, preached a sermon to his fellow colonists. In it he compared their settlement to a "shining city upon a hill" that would serve as a moral exemplar to the world. Ever since, Americans have been inclined to understand the American experiment as "God's effort to make a new beginning in the history of mankind" (466). This sense of exceptionalism profoundly shaped how America saw itself, from Thomas Jefferson's idealized visions of an agrarian society to the notion of Manifest Destiny that drove settlers westward. At midcentury, America was uniquely tempted to see its position at the summit of world power as confirmation of divine favor. For Niebuhr, this was the precise moment that Americans needed an ironic perspective.

Rather than as crusaders for freedom and justice, Niebuhr suggested we see ourselves as the bumbling knight from Miguel de Cervantes's early seventeenth-century classic *Don Quixote de La Mancha*. With his shabby armor, bedraggled steed, and penchant for attacking windmills, Don Quixote cut a ridiculous figure. Yet the sincerity of his ideals exposed the pretensions of feudal society: "While we laugh at the illusions of the bogus knight, we find ourselves laughing with profounder insight at the bogus character of knighthood itself" (472). Like Don Quixote, our self-conception as Americans was at odds with political realities. Granted, Niebuhr concedes, "of all the 'knights' of bourgeois culture, our castle is the most imposing and our horse the most impressive. Our armor is the shiniest . . . and the lady of our dreams is the most desirable." But this comeliness of appearance obscured the ridiculous element in our illusions: "our ideological weapons are frequently as irrelevant as were the spears of the knights, when gunpowder challenged their reign" (475).

And we were locked in combat with a foe more like us than we care to admit, Niebuhr asserted. Communism was a "fierce and unscrupulous Don Quixote on a fiery horse, determined to destroy every knight and lady of civilization" (474). This element of fury derived from the fact that communism gave "one further twist of consistency" to its illusions than we do (473). This rendered communism more effective at translating its misguided ideals into action—and thus, a source of greater political damage. Niebuhr agreed with his contemporaries that communism was profoundly problematic and needed to be resisted, but he insisted that the difference between democratic and communistic forms of civilization was one of degree rather than of kind. While one was clearly preferable to the other, both were in thrall to quixotic illusion. And both bore unwitting witness to the inadequacies of the midcentury world order.

Niebuhr argued that humans could move beyond these illusions by looking at themselves through the lens of irony. For Niebuhr, "Irony consists of apparently fortuitous incongruities in life which are discovered, upon closer examination, to not be fortuitous" (462). On its own, incongruity—that is, the gap between the way things are and the way we expect them to be—was comic. It was the incongruity of the unexpected twist, for instance, that lay at the root of many a well-turned joke. Indeed, irony always contained an element of humor. Yet Niebuhr reminded us that "irony is something more than comedy." In the sense that Niebuhr intended, irony always contains a "hidden element of vanity or pretention": "If virtue becomes vice through some hidden defect in the virtue; if strength becomes weakness because of the vanity to which strength may prompt the mighty man or nation; if security is transmuted into insecurity because too much reliance is placed upon it; if wisdom becomes folly because it does not know its own limits—in all such cases, the situation is ironic" (462).

Irony dissolves once we become aware of it; or rather, irony transforms into either repentance or evil. Confronted with our pretensions, we either repent of them, which presents us with the possibility of grace, or we assert them more forcefully, which leads us down the path of evil. To choose repentance, we cannot take ourselves too seriously. Appreciating the absurdity of our pretensions requires us to have a sense of humor whereby we can discern something of the bumbling Don Quixote in ourselves. It is when we cannot appreciate our own ridiculousness—when we cannot get past our own wounded vanity—that we choose to commit evil rather than repent. Repentance often begins with laughter, and evil with righteous indignation.

Niebuhr proceeded to uncover the ironic elements in the American experience by highlighting the incongruities between the nation's signature achievements and its illusions about what these achievements meant. Here we examine his analysis of American power, innocence, and prosperity.

Power

By virtually every conceivable military, economic, and cultural measure, American might at midcentury was singular. And with the nuclear bomb in its arsenal, the nation possessed a weapon the likes of which humanity had never seen. If any nation ever had the power to enjoy security and shape global destiny, it was the United States.

And yet, the same historical patterns that propelled America to such dizzying heights of dominance also gave rise to the Soviet Union, a formidable opponent with a fundamentally different vision of the route that history should take. Moreover, as of 1949, when the Soviet Union tested its first atomic bomb, both world powers had access to weapons of unprecedented destruction. Thus, at its moment of greatest history-shaping capacity, America was locked in a conflict that had the potential to imperil the very future of the human race. As Niebuhr saw it, "we are drawn into an historic situation in which the paradise of our domestic security is suspended in a hell of global insecurity" (469). The irony of American power at midcentury was that "our own nation . . . is less potent to do what it wants at the hour of its greatest strength than it was in the days of its infancy" (466).

Innocence

The notion of our nation's fundamental innocence is embedded deeply in the American psyche. At our founding we were the nation that "turned its back on the vices of Europe and made a new beginning" (485). We were the land in which prosperity was possible for anyone willing to put in the hard work. We gave the world's tired, its poor, its huddled masses a second chance when no one else would. And we resorted to war only when higher principles were at stake.

How ironic then, Niebuhr observed, that a nation that asserted its innocence so emphatically developed and deployed the atomic bomb: "Thus an 'innocent' nation finally arrives at the ironic climax of its history. It finds itself the custodian of the ultimate weapon which perfectly embodies and symbolizes the ambiguity of physical warfare" (492). The "shining city upon a hill" ushered in the age of nuclear warfare. To meet the challenges of this brave new world it was complicit in creating, "our American nation . . . must slough off many illusions" that had been conceived in the days before it was a superpower. "Otherwise," Niebuhr warned, "we will seek to escape from responsibilities which involve unavoidable guilt, or we will be plunged into avoidable guilt by too great confidence in our virtue" (495). No nation, no matter how great its power or lofty its ideals, could escape the human condition.

Prosperity

Our nation's founders valued happiness — so much so that the Declaration of Independence listed its pursuit as an "inalienable right" (496). And generations of Americans since then have believed that the key to happiness lies in material prosperity. By this logic, midcentury America should have been the happiest nation on earth: "The prosperity of America is legendary. Our standards of living are beyond the dreams of avarice of most of the world. We are a kind of paradise of security and wealth" (497).

And yet, Niebuhr argued, at our seeming moment of triumph, the contradictions of midcentury life "threatened our culture with despair." The same technological prowess that made the 1950s' standard of living possible also made nuclear annihilation possible. Nuclear energy powered homes and bombs alike. Employment was high in part because of the continuing growth of defense industries, the so-called military-industrial complex that fueled the Cold War arms race. Meanwhile, the prosperity that propelled America to a position of world leadership also compelled it to shoulder the burdens of that leadership: "Our confidence in happiness as the end of life, and in prosperity as the basis of happiness is challenged by every duty and sacrifice, every wound and anxiety which our world-wide responsibilities bring upon us" (506). The irony of our prosperity was clear: we attained the wealth that we thought necessary to happiness, only to discover that wealth brings an assortment of new miseries in its wake.

Divine Laughter

In these examples, Niebuhr affirmed that virtue factored into America's rise. He drew attention, however, to the fact that these virtues had not been as pure as we had believed them to be. Irony confronted us with the reality that ulterior motives had insinuated themselves into even the most well-intentioned actions. This point turned Niebuhr's focus toward the theological dimension. "The Biblical view of human nature and destiny," Niebuhr wrote, "moves within the framework of irony with remarkable consistency." The sin of Adam and Eve was to defy the limits God had set for them. Humanity had since replicated this pattern: "All subsequent human actions are infected with a pretentious denial of human limits." The more human beings excelled, the more often they denied their limits. For this reason "the actions of those who are particularly wise or mighty or powerful fall under special condemnation" (578).

True repentance alerted us to the element of comedy in our pretensions, revealed to us in the form of divine laughter. "He that sitteth in the heavens shall laugh," states Psalm 2, because "the people imagine a vain thing." This laughter "has the sting of judgment upon our vanities in it" (510), but it also contained mercy in the form of an invitation to laugh at ourselves. Accepting this invitation allowed us to put our vanity in perspective, which freed us to repent from it. To cultivate the habit of repentance, we had to learn to accept that "the whole drama of human history is under the scrutiny of a divine judge who laughs at human pretensions without being hostile to human aspirations" (576). Irony, in short, could lead to salvation: "Nothing that is worth doing can be achieved in a lifetime; therefore we must be saved by hope. Nothing which is true or beautiful or good makes complete sense of any immediate context of history; therefore we must be saved by faith. Nothing we do, however virtuous, can be accomplished alone; therefore we must be saved by love. No virtuous act is quite as virtuous from the standpoint of our friend or foe as it is from our standpoint. Therefore we must be saved by the final form of love which is forgiveness" (510).

Andrew Bacevich sees profound political implications in Niebuhr's analysis. He discerns a stinging rebuke of a particularly "American form of pride" that drives much of our foreign policy: namely, "that we are innocent, and . . . as an innocent party, we are the injured party. As the innocent party, our motives are not to be questioned." This approach fails to grasp the fundamental truth that "we too are subject to the effects of original sin."

Bacevich also reads Niebuhr as pushing back against the "folly of the United States thinking that it can manage history" that is revealed whenever foreign policy figures use the language of "shaping" a particular region of the world. For Niebuhr, the only one who "knows where the trajectory of history is headed is God" —a fact that we Americans have routinely forgotten in our zeal for projecting our values across the globe. Bacevich summarizes Niebuhr's argument as follows: "Niebuhr would urge us to pay more attention to understanding ourselves. Don't take for granted that we know ourselves. Probe your own motivations. And that really then is the beginning ... of wisdom in foreign policy." Similarly, Mark Massa sees Niebuhr's argument as a reminder that "we're not angels. We're not capable of embodying a pure message apart from the baggage that all human beings, and especially communities of human beings, carry with them." On his read, *The Irony of American History* warns of the "dangers of that heady moment when you think you can do almost anything," and offers us "an extended opportunity to pray for the grace of self-doubt."

Irony attended to an audience different from that of Niebuhr's earlier work. *Moral Man and Immoral Society* and *The Children of Light and the Children of Darkness* were written when American society, or even the world order itself, seemed on the verge of collapse. *The Irony of American History* addressed a nation at the summit of world power. As Bacevich notes, Niebuhr now wrote for a public that, after a "period of some amount of sacrifice, of some amount of want, [is] now able to indulge their desire for new cars, new refrigerators and a new house in the suburb, whatever the case may be." Where previously Niebuhr had preached the imminent collapse of Western civilization, he now articulated how the United States could wield its power with more caution and self-critique in the nuclear age. He also seemed more forgiving of the foibles of democracy and more stridently critical of communism than he used to be.

For certain observers, the fact that he addressed the powerful while consulting in the State Department cemented his reputation as the "establishment theologian." This is not to say that he ceased to be critical. Bacevich argues that Niebuhr was a "profoundly countercultural figure" in the way he took on illusions of innocence and exceptionalism. Elisabeth Sifton maintains that his critical approach created a "penumbra around him of untrustworthy left-winged-ism" that rendered him the subject of FBI vigilance even during his period of greatest influence and acclaim. Yet, as the decade wore on, there did seem to be a change in Niebuhr's tone. Where previously he had emphasized the need for radical transformation, now he emphasized the importance of what Cornel West describes as "slow, organic change" regarding the "manners and moirés of . . . society." Civil rights trailblazers found themselves wondering: Where was Niebuhr the prophetic firebrand when they needed him most? Did Niebuhr's realist emphasis on gradual change favor the status quo at the expense of addressing injustice?

These important questions set the stage for our examination of Niebuhr's legacy in chapter 5. To address them comprehensively, it is essential to establish the context in which Niebuhr was operating in the 1950s and 1960s. We begin with his life-altering health crisis of 1952.

The Stroke

In early 1952, Niebuhr experienced a stroke that left him with slurred speech and impaired mobility. While he was still able to teach, he required a great deal of rest, and needed assistance with everyday tasks. Such a change would have been difficult for anyone, but for Niebuhr, it was soul crushing. For decades he had kept an astonishingly busy schedule. As a former colleague remarked, "Niebuhr put more energy into brushing his teeth in the morning than I would for an entire day's work."[5] Niebuhr suffered from bouts of depression as he struggled to come to terms with the extent to which he now had to rely on others.

The new circumstances required drastic changes within the Niebuhr family as well. Elisabeth recalls, "It was extremely traumatic and very upsetting, and all the old routines were thrown out the door, because a lot of them had built up around my father's extremely active life . . . now he was, at first, bedridden and needing a lot of nursing and medical care, and it changed everything for my mother." Ursula, who was now a professor in the religious studies department at Barnard College, relied on creativity to keep things moving: "She had set up a kind of patchwork quilt arrangement of people who helped keep the show on the road."

Niebuhr still managed to publish at an impressive rate poststroke, due in no small measure to Ursula's work behind the scenes.[6] Healan Gaston notes, "after his stroke and towards the end of his life, she was functioning not so much as his editor, which she had done throughout

5. Quoted in Daniel Rice, *Reinhold Niebuhr and John Dewey: An American Odyssey* (Albany: SUNY Press, 1993), xiv.

6. For more on Ursula's role in Niebuhr's work, see Rebekah Miles, "Uncredited: Was Ursula Niebuhr Reinhold's Coauthor?" *Christian Century*, January 25, 2012.

his lifetime, but even . . . as a virtual co-author." Elisabeth suggests, however, that the nature of their collaboration didn't change as much as one might think: "It's true she came to have a hand in the final preparation of a manuscript, rather more than she had before, but on the other hand she engaged with my father on the theological issues right from the start. . . . [One] ought to think of her hand in *Moral Man and Immoral Society* too."

Yet there was a marked change in the tone and content of Niebuhr's work after his stroke. He nuanced earlier themes, particularly as they pertained to the understanding of history that he had articulated in *Irony*. But he was no longer breaking swaths of new conceptual ground. Part of what had made Niebuhr's voice so distinctive and novel was that he had rooted his reflections in lived experience. Seeing the devastation of the Ruhr region of Germany in the aftermath of World War I firsthand had pushed Niebuhr toward pacifism in the early 1920s. Witnessing the plight of assembly-line workers had prompted him to publicly oppose Ford and make his case for the necessity of coercion in *Moral Man and Immoral Society*. Observing the effects of German bombings while delivering the Gifford Lectures in the United Kingdom had compelled Niebuhr to make a full-throated case for interventionism. And walking the corridors of power had convinced him to warn against the perils of vanity. When the range of his social interactions became more limited following his stroke, so did the scope of his thought.

Yet there was grace to be found in his infirmity. Gaston observes that Niebuhr "benefitted to a certain extent from being forced by circumstances to slow down." Although he and Ursula had always enjoyed a unique rapport, his appreciation for her took on new depth as he came to depend on her more and more. He opened a tribute for their wedding anniversary in 1969 with a fair dose of self-deprecating humor: "38 years ago a young girl from England was united in marriage to a dubious bachelor." He continued, "17 years ago I was stricken with a stroke, the result of compulsive work over the weekends against which she constantly warned. My illness prompted her to give up her beloved teaching, [as] she spent [her] hours as collaborator, editor, and secretary to her benighted husband, and endanger[ed] her health, working 20 hours out of every 24."[7] That Reinhold took the time and effort to type this out amid the various health challenges he confronted in the late 1960s gives us a glimpse into the depths of his gratitude toward Ursula.

7. Reinhold Niebuhr Papers, Library of Congress.

There were also many moments of levity in the poststroke years. Ron Stone, who was Niebuhr's graduate assistant in the 1960s, recalls a heated discussion about marriage and sexuality in one of Reinhold's seminars. Afterward, Niebuhr "confessed that he was impatient with his young, hot-blooded students arguing so much about marriage—the seminar had to move on. He said 'After all, you guys are young and hot-blooded and I'm older with a beautiful younger wife!'" Stone also raised the issue with Ursula: "I remember once a couple of students were pushing Niebuhr in a seminar on his views on marriage, which were very traditional protestant, very conventional. And I chided her after she brought in the soft drinks and beer after one of the seminars, 'Your husband seems terribly conservative on the issue of marriage' and she said, 'Oh, marriage is fun!' and she believed that deeply."

Without the possibility of running off to the next meeting or sermon, Reinhold was also able to connect more with his children, Christopher and Elisabeth. Perhaps he was never quite able to learn "the grace of doing nothing," as H. Richard titled his early 1930s' response to Reinhold regarding the Manchurian crisis. But Reinhold did learn the grace that comes with being forced to slow down. Had he been able to maintain his breakneck pace, he might never have cultivated an interfaith friendship for the ages with the renowned Jewish scholar-activist Rabbi Abraham Heschel.

Abraham Joshua Heschel

Abraham Joshua Heschel was born in Poland in 1907. He pursued his doctoral studies and rabbinical education in Berlin, and continued to live in Germany till the Nazi Gestapo deported him to Poland in 1938. Following the Nazi invasion of Poland, he migrated to the United States in 1940. After the war he accepted a post at Jewish Theological Seminary (JTS) in New York City, where he would remain until his passing in 1972. Heschel established himself as a leading Jewish theologian and philosopher whose influence extended well beyond the orbit of academia: he served as a consultant to Roman Catholicism's Second Vatican Council in the 1960s and became a leading figure in the civil rights movement.

Like Niebuhr, Rabbi Heschel appealed to a broad audience. With titles such as *Man Is Not Alone* (1951), *God in Search of Man* (1955), and *The Prophets* (1962), he helped familiarize a generation of readers with the distinctive features of Jewish thought and conveyed the importance of recovering and utilizing the prophetic tradition of the Hebrew Bible. By the 1960s he had become one of the most well-known religious leaders in the country.

Niebuhr's relationship with Heschel had its roots in a glowing review that Niebuhr wrote of *God in Search of Man* in the April 1, 1951, edition of the *New York Herald Tribune*. The Heschel family treasured this review: Abraham's daughter, Dartmouth professor Susannah Heschel, recalls hearing her parents reference it regularly. Of course, Rabbi Heschel was grateful for the attention it brought to his work. But of far greater significance to him was the fact that such a prominent Christian leader was reading the book of a Jewish author so carefully and perceptively. As Susannah puts it, "For a Christian theologian such as Reinhold Niebuhr to be willing to write a review like this, to be able to understand and appreciate what a Jewish thinker is trying to do, that's extraordinary. In the history of Christian theology, think about it. How often do you find a Christian theologian studying the book of a Jewish theologian and writing with such appreciation and understanding?"

This was all the more extraordinary in light of Abraham Heschel's personal experience. Susannah notes that during his childhood in Poland, young Abraham had learned to "cross the street rather than pass in front of a church" to avoid being harassed by Christian boys. While completing his studies in Germany in the late 1920s and 1930s, Heschel had encountered the disdain with which Christian fellow academics regarded the Jewish Scriptures: "he heard Christian theologians saying that the Old Testament is a Jewish book and should be thrown out of the Christian Bible. He had heard Christian theologians saying Jesus wasn't a Jew. Jesus was an Aryan." He had had to flee Nazism; eventually he had learned that not a single one of his relatives who remained in Nazi-occupied areas survived the Holocaust. In other words, Heschel had encountered Christian anti-Semitism in its full ugliness and horror. Against that backdrop, to have his work understood and appreciated by a figure like Niebuhr meant a great deal.

Shortly after Niebuhr's review of Heschel, the Niebuhrs and the Heschels struck up a friendship. They lived two blocks away from each other on Riverside Drive in Manhattan, so they ran into each other with some regularity. Susannah recalls, "I remember vividly sometimes we would see Dr. Niebuhr across the street at some distance. And my father would point him out because he was tall and distinguished and recognizable and he would say to me even when I was a little girl, 'there goes a great man!'" This made quite the impression on young Susannah. In grammar school, a teacher spent time one day explaining how the class system worked. When the discussion turned to the upper class, Susannah's hand shot up and she exclaimed, "You mean [like] Reinhold Niebuhr!"

The walks that Reinhold and Abraham frequently took together have become the stuff of legend. Years later, Ursula described watching them walk down Riverside Drive, Reinhold "over six feet [tall], leaning a bit like the Tower of Pisa," and Abraham, "a good deal shorter—would he be able to hold Reinhold up if he tilted?" She concluded, "Luckily, Reinhold never did tilt or tumble, but I still have a vivid picture of those two dear figures happily talking to each other with their different architectural conformations."[8] Susannah notes the "mode of the walk": "My father walked rather slowly and he would stop every few yards to talk. So they would walk a bit, stop and talk a bit. Walk a little and stop and talk so it was, it was a walk and a talk and somehow joined . . . a moving talk."

As to what they discussed, one can only speculate. Ursula used to joke that only the Niebuhrs' pet dogs knew. Susannah notes the most likely topics: "I'm sure that they were talking about social and political issues for one thing. I'm sure that as they did that they were discussing passages from the Bible. I'm sure they were talking about prophetic tradition. These were the things that could bind them so easily."

Thinking as they did out of such distinct frameworks, they often disagreed. Susannah notes one such point of disagreement: "One of the central differences is the question of sin and sinfulness. . . . Is there such a thing as an original sin or an inborn desire to sin? My father felt we often have a desire to be deceived to turn away, to be complacent. And he insisted that a religious person can never say I'm a good person because a religious person is always striving to be better . . . but not with a sense of original sinful nature. That would be a place where they would depart." Cornel West observes that Niebuhr and Heschel also had different understandings of how to talk about God. In his earlier writings Niebuhr discussed the "mythic" character of religious language: it uses symbols to help us make sense of our lived experience. Heschel, by contrast, "talks about God as a living God that he has an intuition of." West continues, "When Niebuhr talks

8. See the website On Being with Krista Tippett, accessed October 5, 2016, http://www.onbeing.org/program/moral-man-and-immoral-society-rediscovering-reinhold-niebuhr/feature/notes-friendship.

about the mythic understanding of Christianity, that would drive Heschel crazy. 'The mythic understanding of prophetic Judaism . . . no such thing, Reinhold!' I can see them going at it with a smile over wine."

Life could be lonely for both men. Susannah notes that her father was singularly devoted to his work and saw most forms of socializing as a "waste of time." Reinhold had many friends, but the frenetic pace of his life until his stroke slowed him down left him with precious few opportunities to savor those friendships. Furthermore, it can be difficult for those who possess such an extraordinary combination of spiritual sensitivity and intellectual ability to find others who identify with their particular blessings and burdens. And this is what Reinhold and Abraham found in each other. In 1970, while the Heschels were away in Florida, Ursula recalled Abraham sending a letter to Reinhold that was addressed to his "Beloved and Reverend Friend." He continued, "You are so deeply ingrained in my thoughts, and I am eager to renew our walking and talking together on Riverside Drive."[9] No doubt Reinhold felt the same. Susannah remembers venturing out on her own to visit the Niebuhrs at their second home in Massachusetts shortly before Reinhold died. Even in his bedridden state, "he was so kind and he was so interested and so full of warmth and at the end when I had to leave, he said to me give me a kiss and so I kissed him." She continues, "I felt in that moment that really he loved my father . . . that kiss that he wanted from me was the kiss he wanted to give my father too."

No doubt both men appreciated the irony of a German American pastor and a Polish American rabbi forging such a deep connection. Yet there were striking similarities underlying their cultural and religious differences. West observes, "they both had a sense of humor and humility, and they both had a sense of the underside of the human condition." They each had an abiding appreciation for the Old Testament prophets: their vision of social justice, their withering condemnation of injustice, and their clarion call to hope. And they possessed an extraordinary generosity of spirit toward one another. For his part Heschel trusted Niebuhr because of the way Niebuhr combined advocacy for the Jewish people with proven esteem for Judaism as a religion. Heschel insisted that the religious integrity of Judaism be respected. Susannah notes that her father

9. See the website On Being with Krista Tippett, accessed October 5, 2016, http://www.onbeing.org/program/moral-man-and-immoral-society-rediscovering-reinhold-niebuhr/feature/notes-friendship.

regarded Christian attempts to convert Jews as a form of "spiritual fratricide." When a young man from a Jewish background named Will Herberg confided to Niebuhr that he was considering becoming a Christian, Niebuhr could have easily convinced him to convert. Susannah recollects her father telling the rest of the story: "You know what Niebuhr said to him? He said, go and study Judaism, go become a better Jew." She continues, "for my father this was . . . extraordinary." In Heschel's experience, Christians having this kind of reverence for Judaism was virtually without precedent. By the 1950s Herberg had become one of the preeminent Jewish intellectuals in America. This story clearly illustrates Healan Gaston's observation: "Niebuhr was, at the end of day, a really deeply committed pluralist. His curiosity about people different from himself made him an early proponent of this idea of America as a nation whose democracy was actually not just a Christian project purely, but a Judeo-Christian project, one that was expansive, that would include [not just Jews but] secularists, that would have elements coming from Catholics, that would include a lot of different people." This pluralist streak marks a clear contrast between Niebuhr and the figure who is arguably the true "establishment theologian": the world-renowned Christian evangelist Billy Graham.

Billy Graham

Few religious leaders symbolized and shaped a particular time as Billy Graham did the Cold War era. His revival meetings shattered attendance records at venues all over the world. Biographer Grant Wacker notes that, at a 1973 gathering in Seoul, South Korea, over 1.1 million people gathered to hear Graham speak. This was likely "the largest gathering of humans for a religious purpose in history." From the late 1940s to the first decade of the new century, Graham spoke face-to-face with an estimated 200 million people, and to a television audience of over 2 billion. Over the course of his ministry, over 3 million people submitted "decision cards" at his rallies professing that they had given their lives to Jesus Christ and become born-again Christians. His impact on American culture was such that he became the only living person to be depicted in the stained glass of the National Cathedral in Washington, DC.[10]

10. Grant Wacker, *America's Pastor: Billy Graham and the Shaping of a Nation* (Cambridge, MA: Harvard University Press, Belknap Press, 2014), 21-22.

The Billy Graham phenomenon had its roots in the religious ferment of the postwar era. Andrew Finstuen observes that, as World War II ended and the Cold War began, "people [were] searching for answers, searching for meaning." This prompted them to ask basic existential questions: Who am I? Why am I here? Where am I going? Where is our country going? Why does the world look the way it looks? They looked to religion to help them recover a "sense of certainty and control over their lives after having experienced an out-of-control era." It was in this context that a legendary newspaperman, William Randolph Hearst, heard a handsome, charismatic young preacher in Los Angeles in 1949. He sent his editors a succinct telegram: "Puff Graham"—in other words, give Graham positive publicity. "Soon," observed Jonathan Herzog, "Graham became a household name."[11] Niebuhr wasn't the only religious leader who caught the attention of media moguls; but unlike Niebuhr, Graham managed to remain in their good graces.

Part of Graham's appeal was personal. As Finstuen notes, Graham was "what America wants itself to be . . . he's tall, he's handsome, he dresses well. He seems to embody the economic and optimistic boom in the American psyche." Graham, in short, was the "poster boy for American Christianity." But the clarity and straightforwardness of his message also had appeal. Finstuen summarizes the message: "You've fallen away from Jesus. You're sinners. You need to come forward and accept Jesus Christ as your personal lord and savior. . . . Repent." Although there was some variation from one meeting to the next, the core message remained the same. Such clarity comforted those seeking answers to life's basic questions.

If Graham symbolized middle-American aspirations, he also painted an alluring picture of America as a whole: a God-fearing nation crusading against the godless forces of tyranny; a "shining city upon a hill" dispelling the world's darkness. This portrayal aligned more with Henry Luce and his emphasis on steeling American resolve than with Niebuhr and his insistence on self-criticism. It also gave religious sanction to the vision of American exceptionalism that Niebuhr had confronted in *Irony*.

It was simply a matter of time before Niebuhr would react to Graham. Upon hearing of Graham's upcoming crusade in New York City in 1957, he did. Finstuen notes that, even though the two never met,

---

11. Jonathan Herzog, *The Spiritual-Industrial Complex* (New York: Oxford University Press, 2011), 145.

Niebuhr had a "tortured relationship with Billy Graham." He elaborates, "Niebuhr sees promise in Graham early. He writes a couple of articles. They are critical but he's also trying to push Graham . . . to move out of what he calls 'pietistic individualism,' that is, speaking only directly to individuals. . . . Even though he's ministering to thousands in stadiums, it's all about those few folks who come up, who come forward at the end of a crusade to accept Jesus Christ." Niebuhr felt that Graham's relentless focus on individual Christianity resulted in squandered opportunities to address more broadly systemic injustices in American society: "Niebuhr increasingly gets frustrated with Graham for what he sees as a blindness to other social ills in the United States," states Finstuen. Niebuhr thought that Christians needed to "look at both individuals and systems" in light of the doctrine of sin, whereas Graham "rarely looked at . . . systemic change." For Finstuen, this marks the key difference between them. And it would not be an easy difference to overcome.

Billy Graham's New York City crusade was a tremendous success. In its wake, one might have expected Graham to dismiss Niebuhr as a crotchety seminary professor. Yet in 1958, Graham stated that he had read "nearly everything Mr. Niebuhr has written."[12] Graham saw the value of Niebuhr's critical voice, regardless of whether or not he agreed with Niebuhr's conclusions.

By the end of the decade, Graham had become a national phenomenon. It became commonplace to see Graham at the White House, as he forged connections with one American president after another. In the terms of Graham's evangelical Christian worldview, the logic of these relationships was straightforward: if having one's heart right with God was the foundation of a godly society, then tending to the spiritual needs of the most powerful man in the world was an especially important thing to do. But for Niebuhr, this focus on personal spirituality ignored the possibility that powerful people could use the appearance of piety to sanctify political agendas that were driven more by ego than by principle.

Watching a particularly close relationship develop between Graham and President Richard Nixon prompted Niebuhr to publish a scathing article in 1969 entitled "The King's Chapel and the King's Court." Niebuhr was scandalized, in particular, by the fact that Graham had accepted Nixon's invitation to be the first preacher to speak at the White House's East

---

12. Andrew Finstuen, *Original Sin and Everyday Protestants* (Chapel Hill: University of North Carolina Press, 2009), 62.

Room. Niebuhr took the article's title from the biblical book of Amos, in which the corrupt high priest Amaziah kicked the prophet Amos out of the sanctuary: "O thou seer, go, flee thee away into the land of Judah, and there eat bread, and prophesy there: But prophesy not again any more at Bethel: for it is the king's chapel, and it is the king's court" (Amos 7:12-13 KJV).

"We do not know the architectural proportions of Bethel," Niebuhr noted. "But we do know that it is, metaphorically, the description of the East Room of the White House, which President Nixon has turned into a kind of sanctuary." By bringing Graham to the White House, Nixon had not only violated the principle of separation of church and state enshrined in the Bill of Rights; he had also created a convenient way of co-opting the religious authority of those he invited to speak. "It is wonderful," Niebuhr wrote acidly, "what a simple White House invitation will do to dull the critical faculties, thereby confirming the fears of the Founding Fathers."

The significance of Graham's being the first person to preach in the East Room was not lost on Niebuhr. Graham had grown so close to Nixon that Niebuhr perceived them as sharing the same basic understanding of the relationship between religion and politics. The "Nixon-Graham doctrine," as he called it, had two main defects. First, it "regards all religion as virtuous in guaranteeing public justice." It therefore failed to distinguish between religion that pays lip service to power and religion that critiques power. Second, it "assumes that a religious change of heart, such as occurs in an individual conversion, would cure men of all sin." It therefore overlooked the ways in which converted individuals continue to be part of sinful social structures. But he saved his most stinging indictment for the end. Quoting Amos 5:24—" But let justice roll down like waters, and righteousness like an everflowing stream" (RSV)—he noted that this was a "favorite text of the late Martin Luther King." "It is unfortunate that he was murdered before he could be invited to that famous ecumenical congregation in the White House. But on second thought, the question arises: would he have been invited? Perhaps the FBI, which spied on him, had the same opinion of him as Amaziah had of Amos."[13]

He closed by directly comparing Amaziah to FBI head J. Edgar Hoover. It came as little surprise, then, that the FBI reopened Niebuhr's

---

13. Reinhold Niebuhr, "The King's Chapel and the King's Court," *Christianity and Crisis* (August 4, 1969), 211-12.

file. Hoover included a memo calling Niebuhr a "Christian Revolutionary" and ordering his investigators to keep looking for ways to link Niebuhr to communism.[14] He did not appear to register the irony of how this reaction reinforced Niebuhr's comparison of him with Amaziah. Ron Stone relates how he received his first death threat for a letter he wrote defending the article to the editor of a Pittsburgh newspaper. Niebuhr later told Stone that he received a "bushel of hate mail" afterward, which, according to Ursula, "rather pleased him."[15] Niebuhr seemed to have anticipated that there would be consequences for taking on a president, the nation's most beloved religious leader, and the director of the FBI in such direct and castigating fashion.

The way Nixon's time in the White House ended vindicated Niebuhr's critique. When the Watergate scandal broke in the early 1970s, Graham defended Nixon almost until the end. Andrew Finstuen points out that not until the White House tapes were made public and Graham heard evidence of Nixon's profanity-laden manipulation behind the scenes, did he finally feel "utterly embarrassed and ashamed for his association with Nixon." From that point forward, he was "a little more cautious . . . about how close he became to presidents."

Not all of Niebuhr's criticisms were fair. There was an element of caricature to Niebuhr's depiction of Graham, much as there had been in his portrayal of the Social Gospel in the 1930s or of Barth in the 1940s. But Graham appeared to have realized the element of truth intertwined with the caricature. As he put it in the 1980s: "Look, I need some more Reinhold Niebuhrs in my life. I would say Reinhold Niebuhr was a great contributor to me. He helped me work through some of my problems."[16] Graham did not specify what the "problems" were. But one wonders if Niebuhr's words helped him think through his relationship to political power. It was Graham, after all, who informed the way that multiple presidents understood the relationship between faith and politics. Niebuhr may have been labeled "establishment theologian," but it was Graham who fulfilled the role.

Niebuhr was not the "insider" he is often portrayed to have been. As

14. See Ronald Stone, *Professor Reinhold Niebuhr: A Mentor to the Twentieth Century* (Louisville: Westminster John Knox, 1992), 182.

15. Richard Wightman Fox, *Reinhold Niebuhr: A Biography* (Ithaca, NY: Cornell University Press, 1996), 282.

16. See Andrew Finstuen, "The Prophet and the Evangelist," *Books and Culture* (July/August 2006), http://www.booksandculture.com/articles/2006/julaug/3.8.html.

Robin Lovin comments, "if you ask 'Who's the general public going to identify as *the* religious voice?' well it's going to be Billy Graham, Norman Vincent Peale . . . the people Niebuhr complains about in his writings." But as the case of Graham illustrates, Niebuhr did succeed in being a voice of conscience to those who were in the positions of greatest power and influence.

John Courtney Murray

As a general rule, Niebuhr was hardest on those to whom he was the most similar. As David Brooks observes, "There was never a group he was part of that he was not the deepest critic of. And he loved to criticize his own, whether it's German-Americans, whether it's Progressives, or whether it's Americans. Or whether it's Christians." Yet he was quite generous in his assessment of those whose background and beliefs were clearly different from his own. As much as Niebuhr and Heschel had in common, they were practitioners of different faiths. Some of Niebuhr's most vocal admirers, such as Supreme Court Justice Felix Frankfurter or Harvard historians Perry Miller and Arthur Schlesinger Jr., were atheists. Niebuhr's interaction with them made it clear that the admiration was mutual.

This raises the question of Niebuhr's relationship to Catholicism. Was it primarily critical, as was his relationship to the Social Gospel or evangelical Christianity? Or was it appreciative, as was his relationship to his Jewish or atheist colleagues? Tellingly, the answer appears to be somewhere in the middle.

Catholicism occupies a complicated space in the American story. On the one hand, Catholics founded the Maryland Colony in 1632, and since the 1850s they have formed the largest Christian subgroup on US soil. On the other hand, for much of American history Catholics have been the target of suspicion and vicious discrimination on the part of the Protestant majority (anti-Catholicism, for instance, helped fuel the Ku Klux Klan's massive resurgence in certain parts of the country in the 1920s). The status of Catholics in America improved drastically in the post–World War II era, as various Catholic immigrant groups such as the Irish and Italians became integrated with mainstream society.

But key differences remained between Catholic and Protestant forms of Christianity. Catholicism had a centralized church structure; Protestantism was largely decentralized. Catholicism emphasized historic church teaching alongside the Bible, whereas many Protestant communities proclaimed that they recognized only the Bible's authority. These differences had far-reaching implications for the ways in which Protestants and Catholics understood the relationship between religion and society.

Enter Jesuit priest John Courtney Murray. If Niebuhr introduced the notion of original sin to American politics and culture, Murray did something similar for the natural law tradition in Catholicism. Murray's ability to communicate the relevance of natural law to the pluralist midcentury American context landed him on the cover of *Time* magazine in 1960. Murray's success was all the more remarkable because he emerged out of what Lisa Cahill calls the "American Catholic immigrant experience": "Catholics arrived as a lower class. They were not part of the dominant Protestant mainstream culture and they had to struggle very hard as immigrants and as Catholics to be heard, to be accepted as valued contributors to the mainstream discourse." Yet, by the time Murray appeared on *Time*'s cover, he and Niebuhr had established themselves, in the words of Mark Massa, as the "two great giants of their respective traditions."

The natural law tradition has roots extending back to ancient Greece. It presupposes that the universe has a moral structure that human beings are wired to comprehend. Specifically Christian variants of natural law maintain that, while sin marred the ability of human beings to behave according to these precepts, their God-given capacity to perceive right and wrong remains largely intact. Beginning in the Middle Ages, Catholicism developed a rich social theory on the basis of natural law. Yet the natural law tradition had not been updated to accommodate the sweeping social changes of the twentieth century. Murray made a case for how natural law supplied a framework for achieving moral consensus in the pluralistic and democratic context of mid-twentieth-century America.

Niebuhr and Murray were good friends who enjoyed bantering back and forth in private as well as in public. They seem to have recognized in one another a helpful foil for their respective positions. Niebuhr thought that natural law theories risked investing our provisional sense of how the ways of God map onto human affairs with a morally dangerous aura of permanence. For instance, it can be difficult for the modern mind to comprehend why medieval Europeans (or New England Puritans, for that matter) put people to death on charges of witchcraft. Yet those responsible often saw themselves as doing right by their particular understanding of a universally binding moral code. Similarly, future generations may see our own judgments of right and wrong as misguided, however clear the moral stakes seem to us now. For his part, Murray thought that Niebuhr's Christian realism became too easily mired in ambiguity to make crucial moral distinctions. In its concern over investing human judgments with too much moral authority, Murray believed, Christian realism deprived us of necessary resources for enacting a viable form of common morality in a democratic context.

Other differences between the two thinkers were also significant. Mark Massa observes that "they disagreed . . . profoundly on the ways in which human beings could know the ends of acts or the goodness or badness of acts based upon a reading of the natural world." Yet their disagreements weren't as stark as they sometimes seemed. As Cahill observes, "They both believed in the power of grace and justice in history and they were also very aware of evil and sin. And also the relativity and provisional character of any particular diagnosis of the human situation. But they emphasized different aspects of the big picture." Cahill notes that whereas Niebuhr emphasized "sin as a barrier" to achieving consensus based on an "intimation of the objectively true and good," Murray argued that natural law provided a viable basis for attaining this consensus. While this difference in emphasis has important implications for ethics, Cahill concludes, "I don't think that either one of them really overlooked the other side."

Niebuhr's ongoing dialogue with Murray no doubt contributed to his deepening appreciation for the role that Catholicism played in American life. When the public questioned whether a practicing Catholic such as John F. Kennedy could make a good president, Niebuhr went on record stating that Kennedy's Catholic faith should not be made into a campaign issue. Indeed, Niebuhr privately questioned whether Kennedy took his faith seriously enough.[17] This may not seem particularly noteworthy in retrospect. But at the time, many voters wondered whether a Catholic president's religious obedience to the pope would supersede loyalty to country. By defending Kennedy's faith, Niebuhr was confronting significant elements of anti-Catholic sentiment that lingered in mainstream American society.

Incidentally, one of Niebuhr's final published articles, "Toward New Intra-Christian Endeavors," contained a sustained reflection on Catholicism. He acknowledged that his "high-handed stance" toward Cathol-

---

17. Fox, *Reinhold Niebuhr: A Biography*, 271.

icism earlier in his career had been mistaken on various points.[18] The Second Vatican Council had recently concluded, introducing sweeping changes into Catholic thought and practice such as saying Mass in the vernacular (previously, the Catholic Mass was only said in Latin) and emphasizing the value of ecumenical dialogue between the Catholic Church and other churches and religious groups. Murray had been deeply involved in the council's proceedings, and perhaps Niebuhr's relationship with Murray had given him renewed appreciation for what Catholicism had to offer. In the closing paragraph he wrote, "The new ecumenical spirit between Protestants and Catholics will profit by a new appreciation of the values both branches of Christendom have in common —though one branch may emphasize unity and order while the other emphasizes liberty."[19] As distinct branches of the same Christian faith, Catholicism and Protestantism had much to learn from one another. Their differences did not need to be a source of antagonism; they could also be the basis of mutual strengthening. It is safe to say that Niebuhr's lively yet cordial conversations with John Courtney Murray helped him arrive at this conclusion.

Committed to Engagement

As his relationships with Heschel, Graham, and Murray demonstrate, Niebuhr was committed to in-depth engagement across the religious and ideological spectrum. In these engagements he modeled a particular vision of what it meant both to be a committed Christian and to be thoroughly invested in the pluralistic democratic project. His ability to speak to the concerns of a secular audience was on display in an appearance on the *Mike Wallace Interview*, which aired in the spring of 1958.[20] The interview placed Niebuhr in elite company: over the two-year run of the show, various prominent figures, from Salvador Dali and Frank Lloyd Wright to Eleanor Roosevelt and Henry Kissinger, appeared opposite host Mike Wallace, who would go on to become a longtime anchor of *60 Minutes*.

Wallace opened by introducing his guest: "This is Dr. Reinhold

18. Reinhold Niebuhr, "Toward New Intra-Christian Endeavors," *Christian Century*, December 31, 1969, 1663.

19. Niebuhr, "Toward New Intra-Christian Endeavors," 1667.

20. *The Mike Wallace Interview*, April 27, 1958. The Harry Ranson Center at the University of Texas has made video of the interview available at http://www.hrc.utexas.edu/collections/film/holdings/wallace/.

Niebuhr, a Protestant minister, one of the most important and challenging religious thinkers in the world. Dr. Niebuhr is a critic of America's religious revival and he says that religion will not necessarily vanquish injustice or communism." As would any good interviewer, Wallace presented Niebuhr in a way that piqued the curiosity of a midcentury audience: A minister who criticized revival? Who *questioned* the way that our leaders invoked God? Six years after his stroke, Niebuhr lacked the fiery dynamism of his younger self; however, his observations retained their incisive edge.

Early in the interview Wallace turned to the unprecedented religiosity of the time: "With church attendance increasing, college students returning to religion, the apparent success of the evangelists . . . in large measure you have criticized this revival. Why?" Niebuhr responded, "I wouldn't criticize the whole revival. I've criticized the revival wherever it gives petty and trivial answers to very great and ultimate questions about the meaning of our life." In other words, Niebuhr felt that certain sectors of the revival made it seem as if accepting Jesus and going to church was the only thing in life that mattered. But religious conversion did not magically make us wiser in our political decision making. We still needed to think carefully about how to relate faith and politics.

Wallace then pivoted to the question of how religious language had been invoked in the Cold War: "We're constantly being told, Dr. Niebuhr, by our political and by our church leaders, that in our fight against Communism, we are on God's side, that we're God-fearing people, they are atheists . . . and therefore we must ultimately win. What about that?"

Niebuhr responded, "All this talk about atheistic materialism and God-fearing Americans, I think is beside the point. It's a rather vapid form of religion." He pointed out, "In the Old Testament, the God of the Prophets never was completely on Israel's side." This often-overlooked aspect of Israel's relationship with God deprived us of being able to claim God for our own cause: "if you equate God's judgment with your judgment, you have a wrong religion."

The main issue that Niebuhr saw with communism was not its atheism, but its worship of the false god of human progress—the same accusation Niebuhr had made of certain forms of liberalism. He believed that the way forward in our relations with the Soviet Union was to acknowledge that we live under a "common predicament," namely, the nuclear dilemma. This would help put our differences into perspective, however serious they might be.

By refusing to frame the conflict in terms of godliness versus godlessness, Niebuhr pushed his listeners to think about the Cold War in a more nuanced way. Communism worshiped a false god, but democracy-loving Americans were also vulnerable to idolatry. When we claimed to enact the will of God through our politics, we engaged in a no less egregious form of idol worship. Niebuhr's articulation of the nuclear dilemma as a common predicament evoked another, more universal "common predicament": original sin. Like the Soviets, Americans were deeply flawed beings making our way in a broken world. And we were in no less need of divine mercy and forgiveness than they.

Wallace concluded by observing, "Reinhold Niebuhr is a man of God, but a man of the world as well. Dr. Niebuhr would seem to be saying that if a nation would survive and remain free, its citizens must use religion as a source of self-criticism, not as a source of self-righteousness."

This was an apt description of Niebuhr and an astute summary of his Cold War–era message. As a nation, we wanted to see ourselves as a paragon of righteous strength, like the medieval crusader-king Richard the Lionheart. But true religion ought to remind us that we had more in common with the bumbling Don Quixote.

CHAPTER FIVE

Niebuhr and the
Twenty-First-Century Conscience

O n June 4, 1971, two hundred people gathered at First Congregational Church in Stockbridge, Massachusetts, to pay their respects to one of America's great public intellectuals. In keeping with Niebuhr's humble Midwestern roots, the memorial service was a modest affair. Among those asked to speak that day was Rabbi Abraham Joshua Heschel.[1]

This likely came as little surprise to those who knew Reinhold well —who had seen him and Heschel walking together on Riverside Drive, or had read Reinhold's glowing reviews of Heschel's work. But some others—Stockbridge residents who knew Niebuhr in passing, or those who knew him by his "establishment" reputation but had not bothered to read much of what he wrote—may have been left scratching their heads. A Jewish rabbi giving the eulogy for one of the day's most prominent Christian clergymen?

The strangeness of the moment was not lost on the Heschel family. Susannah Heschel recalls, "It was during one of their walks on Riverside drive a few years earlier that Reinhold Niebuhr asked my father to deliver the eulogy at his funeral. My father told me and . . . we were all taken aback. Because here was a great Christian theologian who must know Christian pastors to ask. Why a Jew?"

One reason, of course, is that they were close friends and colleagues. Another is that they were both lifelong scholars of religion. As Elisabeth Sifton puts it, "they're two elderly gentlemen who appreciate liturgical problems like who would preach at what funeral." They eventually came

---

1. Richard Wightman Fox, *Reinhold Niebuhr: A Biography* (Ithaca, NY: Cornell University Press, 1996), 292–93.

to an understanding: "they pledged to each other that they would each do that, whoever came first that they would eulogize each other." But the request also had profound historical and theological implications. Susannah observes, "Asking my father, in itself, is something of great historical moment. Think about that: in 2000 years did Christian theologians ask a Jew to deliver the eulogy? For the greatest Christian theologian of America of the twentieth century, a Jew gives the eulogy." Yet the request befitted Reinhold Niebuhr. It was a way of both honoring a cherished friend and making a weighty ecumenical statement: that Christians and Jews shared common theological convictions, and thus, could mutually understand one another, even if they did not always agree. Even in his death, Niebuhr pointed to a cause greater than himself.

Rabbi Heschel's words that day rang with personal warmth and poetic beauty:

> For many of us the world will be darker without you. Reinhold Niebuhr, your spirituality combined heaven and earth, as it were. Your life was an example of one who did justly, loved mercy and walked humbly with his God, an example of unity of worship and living. You reminded us that evil will be conquered by the One, while you stirred us to help conquer evils one by one.
>
> . . . His legacy is rich, precious, vital: Purity of heart, disgust with intellectual falsehood, with spiritual sham, whether in the Congress or in our own sanctuaries. . . . How shall we thank you, Reinhold Niebuhr, for the light you have brought into our lives? For the strength you have given to our faith? For the wisdom you have imparted in our minds?
>
> . . . He appeared among us like a sublime figure out of the Hebrew Bible. Intent on intensifying responsibility, he was impatient of excuse, contemptuous of pretense and self-pity. . . . Niebuhr's life was a song in the form of deeds, a song that will go on forever.[2]

There is no question that Niebuhr was a great figure. In deeds as well as words, he bore eloquent witness to both the hope-giving and disquieting powers of faith. For countless contemporaries he was a spur to

---

2. Abraham Joshua Heschel, "Eulogy for Reinhold Niebuhr," On Being with Krista Tippett, accessed October 13, 2016, http://www.onbeing.org/program/moral-man-and-immoral-society-rediscovering-reinhold-niebuhr/extra/reinhold-niebuhr-timel-47.

moral action, a source of moral guidance, and a uniquely insightful critic. Yet present-day readers are left with the questions: What does Niebuhr offer us today, as we confront the dilemmas of our own time and place? Does Niebuhr's message retain its unsettling power, or does it lose something essential without his dynamism and charisma to animate it? Does Niebuhr continue to help us understand and respond to the ethical terrain of our world, or is his legacy bound by the historical events that spurred his thought?

No one who was interviewed for this project disputes his influence. As Stanley Hauerwas puts it, Niebuhr "may be so much in the drinking water that it's very hard to avoid thinking the way he has taught you to think, even though you don't know that it is Niebuhr that taught you to think that." There is disagreement, however, over which aspects of his legacy continue to be valuable and which are better left in the past. Views run the gamut: Cornel West praises the daring radicalism of Niebuhr's early works and questions the gradualist tendencies of his later works. David Brooks lauds Niebuhr's personal courage and realism about power politics but thinks he placed too much emphasis on self-criticism. Hauerwas states flatly, "I have trouble thinking of any place I agree with him."

This chapter places the voices of our interviewees in conversation with one another with two questions in mind: What was Niebuhr's legacy? And how does Niebuhr speak to us today? We begin by examining what two of our interviewees said about their initial attraction to Niebuhr.

Two Case Studies

The American president most deeply influenced by Niebuhr knew him only through his writings. Jimmy Carter recalls encountering Niebuhr's thought during his days in the navy: "I was idealistic, and I knew that my time as a submarine officer was dedicated to combat and defending our country with my life if necessary. And how to combine that willingness to take a practical approach to any threat to our country on the one hand, and to fulfill the teachings of Jesus Christ who is the Prince of Peace on the other hand was difficult for me to assimilate. And then I began to hear about Reinhold Niebuhr."[3]

---

3. Journey Films interview with Jimmy Carter, July 13, 2016. Unless otherwise noted, subsequent quotes attributed to Carter are from this interview.

Niebuhr's trademark ambivalence, his ability to hold two conflicting ideas in tension, appealed to Carter as he grappled with the implications of being both a Christian and a member of the US military. As Carter's career took a political turn, Niebuhr's words continued to give him inspiration: "I quoted him quite often, and one of the quotes I remember . . . 'the sad duty of politics is to establish justice in a sinful world.' And I faced a sinful world and a challenging world, but I wanted to do the best I could as a politician to establish justice in that world that was beyond my control." Particularly when facing complicated decisions as president, Carter recalls, "my subconscious was always going back to Niebuhr and his teaching to help me explain the quandary of the situation that I faced."

Politicians are by no means the only public figures who have found inspiration in Niebuhr. He is also inspiring to those who analyze the political process. David Brooks recalls first encountering Niebuhr while on an international assignment. He picked up a copy of *The Irony of American History*, and after reading it, found that he perceived the events unfolding around him in a new and more incisive light:

> I was a *Wall Street Journal* correspondent in Europe in the middle of a lot of historic events — the end of the Cold War, the reunification of Germany, the creating of the Maastricht Treaty, to attempt to unify Europe, and so there were these big historic events. Some of them were tremendously idealistic and there was a sense that history was coming to an end, that there was going to be a reign of goodness and peace and unification . . . and somehow something struck me awry about that, that human history was probably not coming to an end, that human nature probably hadn't changed. And here was Niebuhr . . . saying, you know, the nature of man is such that we can't expect an end to conflict, we can't expect an end to egotism and to pride. And some of these illusions that we can create a peaceful, unified Europe are nice illusions, but it may not work out that way.

Brooks realized that the power of Niebuhr's analysis was the product, not merely of his astute political observations, but of the way he brought ethics to bear on politics: "he was seeing politics through a moral lens. . . . I found that deeper and more profound lens much more explanatory of what's actually happening."

Carter and Brooks are a study in contrasts: a member of the GI generation and a baby boomer; a Democrat and a Republican; a submarine officer who would become commander in chief and a journalist who would become a prominent cultural critic; a Southern Baptist and a New York Jew. And yet at key junctures in their respective lives and careers, they were both drawn to Niebuhr's guiding light. In today's polarized political climate, a figure that retains appeal across divides of generation, politics, culture, and religion is worth noting.

But what lies at the heart of Niebuhr's appeal? Does he still challenge people to see the world differently, or does he give them the tools they need to make their peace with the world as they find it? Is he a prophetic voice, or an apologist for the status quo? Our contributors offer a range of opinions on this question. Setting them in conversation creates a nuanced account of Niebuhr's legacy as a flawed yet vital thinker with potential to stir consciences and enrich public discourse in the twenty-first century.

The Niebuhr Legacy

As a big-picture thinker, Niebuhr had a way of addressing several topics at once. This makes it difficult to tease out and analyze one particular strand of his thought. Any such effort risks losing sight of how that strand interweaves with other aspects of his vision. Below, I assess his legacy in three arenas. The first is politics, which, in Niebuhr's view, deals primarily with questions of how to ethically wield power, especially the power of governments. The second is society, which entails questions about how human beings relate to one another. Here Niebuhr is primarily interested in how the categories of love and justice shape human relations. The third arena is religion, which, for Niebuhr, deals primarily with how humans find meaning in life. There is considerable overlap among the categories, as they are inextricably intertwined in Niebuhr's vision. Nevertheless, using these categories can still help to bring analytical clarity to our assessment of his legacy.

Politics

It is no coincidence that many of Niebuhr's admirers began to take his thought seriously when they were confronted with the challenges of wielding power. We see an example of this in Jimmy Carter. More recently, both John McCain and Barack Obama cited Niebuhr as one of their favorite thinkers in the lead-up to the 2008 presidential election.

Part of Niebuhr's appeal derives from his appreciation for both the necessity and the ambiguity of power. Those who sense this tension find in Niebuhr a thinker who can help them wrestle with power's moral implications. In Gary Dorrien's view, Niebuhr helps them address the question: "What does it mean for me to exercise this power in a morally responsible way?"

For Niebuhr, to use power responsibly, we have to temper its exercise with self-criticism. As David Brooks puts it, "You are trying to take action while being reminded by Reinhold Niebuhr of your own weaknesses and your own tendency to be carried away by your own righteousness." Niebuhr modeled this approach in his own political life: "he'll go into the mud when he needs to, for good purposes, but not with any relish, with a lot of self-suspicion."

While Brooks appreciates Niebuhr's caution, he also thinks he focuses too much on self-critique: "He's always a man on a gray horse: Let's go forward, but not too fast. Let's take action, but not too aggressively. Let's have some confidence, but not too much. And so he's always folding back in on himself." Put otherwise: Niebuhr does not permit power brokers the luxury of an easy conscience. He is too aware of power's role in accomplishing good to forgo its use, and too aware of power's corrupting character to relish its use.

The rationale for Niebuhr's position comes back to his faith. Even in its most "secular" variants, his political philosophy—Christian realism—is steeped in notions of sin and grace. Niebuhr thought human beings sought their own well-being at the expense of others. This sinful tendency runs so deep that it insinuates itself into even our best intentions. Consequently, the exercise of power is always infected by this element of self-seeking. This is true no matter how righteous our cause or how terrible the enemy. To relish the exercise of power is to downplay the pervasiveness of sin: to forget that "the evil in the foe is the evil in the self," as Healan Gaston reminds us.

But for Niebuhr, the "evil in the self" is precisely what power tempts us to forget. Foolish children of light that we are, power makes us confident in our righteousness and the purity of our motives. And this causes us to lose touch with political reality. Only by committing to a process of perpetual self-critique and repentance do we remain rooted enough in reality to use power in a morally responsible way. What Brooks sees as an overly tentative posture, Niebuhr saw as a vital safeguard against our propensity for selfishness and self-destructiveness.

Niebuhr recognized that perpetual self-criticism without a counterbalance could lead us to despair. Niebuhr repeatedly referenced the seventeenth-century French philosopher Blaise Pascal's language of the "glory and misery of man." For Niebuhr, a good political philosophy needed to do justice to both facets of human existence—the glory and the misery—and needed theological language to do so. Using the language of sin to draw out the misery of human existence was a necessary corrective to the tendency of the powerful to trumpet their successes and downplay their failings. But Niebuhr also believed that we need to balance this awareness of the depths of human misery with a vision of the heights of human glory. To grasp this vision, it is not enough to dream of self-determination or a world free of want; we need hope in redemption. As Lisa Cahill notes, "Christian realism starts with a realistic appraisal of the human situation, but in light of Christian faith and hope does believe it can be transformed."

Niebuhr's invocations of hope offer us insight into the theological dimension of his political philosophy. For Niebuhr, the fact that human beings are able to accomplish so much good even in their broken state provides a tantalizing glimpse of human potential. Even the glimpse is intoxicating enough to make us dream of a better world in which all human beings live in harmony. But our utopian visions never pan out, because the self-sabotaging tendencies of our sinful nature run too deep. Human brokenness simply cannot sustain human greatness.

This does not mean that our visions of greatness are illusory. We simply need to be healed before we are capable of enacting these visions. This full healing comes at the end of history, when God brings mercy and justice into perfect harmony at the final judgment. In the meantime, cultivating a posture of repentance in our politics allows divine grace to enter our actions in ways that we don't necessarily understand or even perceive. And we go about our attempts to build greater harmony in a broken world in the hope that our political efforts are "in the hands of a Divine Power," whose "suffering love can overcome the corruptions of [human] achievements, without negating the significance of our striving."[4]

---

4. Reinhold Niebuhr, "The Children of Light and the Children of Darkness," in *Reinhold Niebuhr: Major Works on Religion and Politics*, ed. Elisabeth Sifton (New York: Library of America, 2015), 458.

Back to Brooks's analogy: the man on the gray horse counterbalances self-criticism with the hope that even his failings will be redeemed. This hope generates the "sublime madness in the soul" that propels him forward.[5] If an awareness of sin generates the habit of repentance, a vision of redemption keeps us committed to political engagement. According to Robin Lovin, the question always underlying Niebuhr's politics is: "how do you reconcile ultimate loyalty to God with the demands that are made on you as a member of a human political community?" Niebuhr's attempts to answer this question offer a model for engaging in politics with both self-critique and hope.

While Brooks believes that Niebuhr places too much emphasis on self-criticism, others argue that Niebuhr is not nearly self-critical enough. Stanley Hauerwas argues that Niebuhr completely misunderstands what the Christian role in politics should be. Niebuhr "gives you a sense that you know the way the world is and you have a role in it," and "makes you a hard-headed player in the world in which we find ourselves as a Christian." Coming from a pacifist, this is not a compliment. For Hauerwas, Niebuhr seduces his readers into participating in the very cycles of violence from which God seeks to redeem us. This prompts Hauerwas to define Christian realism as "Niebuhr's articulation of the necessity of violence in a world of deep injustice to achieve relative political ends."

Lisa Cahill reads Niebuhr differently. She does not see him as discrediting Christian faith, or even as trying to "retain a credibility of Christian vocabulary" in the political arena. Rather, she interprets him as attempting to "prevent that vocabulary from being used in the service of collective egoism. And division, factionalism, betrayal of the common good, and forgetting those who have less a voice." Niebuhr, in other words, seeks to equip others to nudge a broken world incrementally toward justice.

This raises another important aspect of Niebuhr's political approach: how power comes into play in democratic politics. For Niebuhr, the notion of checks and balances was especially well suited to human nature. It acknowledged the inescapable tendency to act according to self-interest, and it supplied mechanisms through which individuals and collectives could negotiate the balance of power. A well-constructed system of checks and balances sets the power of one group against the power of

---

5. Reinhold Niebuhr, "Moral Man and Immoral Society," in Sifton, *Reinhold Niebuhr: Major Works*, 350.

another group in a way that would "beguile, deflect, harness and re-strain self-interest, individual and collective, for the sake of the community."[6] The democratic system would mitigate the potential damage of unchecked power by providing mechanisms through which those with lesser power could hold those with greater power accountable. This, in turn, would carve out social space for human good to flourish.

In its sensitivity to the need to balance power, this approach is rooted in a Christian view of human nature. As Cahill points out, "the doctrine of sin reminds us that there has to be a balance of power and that those who are not currently part of the [political] discourse need to be included." This balance of power is what makes the movement toward justice and human flourishing possible. For Cahill, Niebuhr's political vision as a whole is rooted both in awareness of "the universality of pride, the disguising of pride by noble ideals that we proclaim," and in the "importance of never giving up, of always realizing that we can make our society and the world we live in a better place." Andrew Finstuen summarizes this approach as follows: "never forget the levels of sin and the levels of virtue that encompass you as a human being."

Niebuhr's understanding of power and coercion in politics has its shortcomings. He is often criticized for being too preoccupied with the effects of sin for his vision of the human potential for good to come through. Even his most charitable interpreters find it lacking at points. Cahill notes that Niebuhr's version of Christian realism could be "pragmatic to a fault." Mark Massa thinks that he "overplays the sin a little bit and underplays the grace a little bit." But Niebuhr does manage to expose the inadequacy of political visions that neglect to take theological perspectives into account. In Massa's view, this is part of why he holds perennial appeal for those in power: "People who go on to be important players in the United States and in world history ... discover Reinhold Niebuhr and say, 'This is something I need to take seriously and think about here.'" The ambiguous nature of power makes a bit more sense when we hold both the glory and the misery of being human in tension.

---

6. Niebuhr, "The Children of Light," in Sifton, *Reinhold Niebuhr: Major Works*, 378.

Society

When Union Theological Seminary brought Niebuhr onto its faculty in the late 1920s, he was hired to teach ethics. Part of what made him such a compelling figure in those earlier years was that he practiced what he preached. He threw himself into local politics, spoke at meetings all over the city, and provided advice and support to students' attempts to agitate on behalf of social justice causes. Under Niebuhr's influence, activism at Union flourished—in the eyes of some, to the detriment of theological education. In his biography of Dietrich Bonhoeffer, Charles Marsh relates Bonhoeffer's frustration with what he saw as a flippant attitude toward theology at Union: "One day, after a lively class discussion, Bonhoeffer approached Niebuhr and asked in exasperation, 'Is this a theological school or a school for politicians?'"[7]

Bonhoeffer's point was that theological education needed to be taken more seriously in the American context. But the question could also be interpreted to suggest a clear dividing line between theological discourse and social issues. For Niebuhr, no such dividing line existed. As Marsh observes, "Niebuhr professed that the question of how to be in the world—how one analyzes the contemporary social situation and responds to its needs and conflicts—mattered more to theology than all the parsing of sacred doctrines."[8] In his unremitting passion for social justice, Niebuhr remained very much within the Social Gospel tradition of early twentieth-century Baptist pastor and theologian Walter Rauschenbusch. Hauerwas observes that Niebuhr "may have criticized Walter Rauschenbusch, but he was always deeply concerned for the poor." For Massa, "Reinhold Niebuhr was the last of the liberal Social Gospelers."

Niebuhr's approach to social ethics derives its dynamism from the way he relates the categories of love and justice. In the early 1930s Niebuhr criticized the Social Gospel for presuming that the ethic of Jesus, rooted in perfect sacrificial love, could be actualized in history. "Love perfectionism," as Niebuhr called it, shattered in its confrontation with a sinful world. Pure sacrificial love would always wind up crucified.

This is not to deny the reality of love. Rather, it is to assert that we must begin our ethics by acknowledging that our love is rendered imper-

---

7. Charles Marsh, *Strange Glory: A Life of Dietrich Bonhoeffer* (New York: Vintage Books, 2015), 106.

8. Marsh, *Strange Glory*, 106.

fect by sin. We see evidence of this imperfection in the way that conflict seeps in to even our most intimate and loving relationships. If enacting perfect love proves impossible in our immediate relationships, how could we possibly pretend to enact perfect love in society?

Justice, for Niebuhr, is the mechanism through which love manifests in a sinful world. The very notion of justice presupposes that human relations exist in a state of conflict. Were they to exist in a state of perfect harmony, appeals to justice simply would not be necessary. The fact that all human societies have notions of justice attests to the reality of sin; yet the fact that we are able to refine and improve our justice systems—that we can advance the cause of justice—points to the enduring power of love. Indeed, if we stopped striving after an ideal of love, the social gains achieved through justice would evaporate. Justice reminds us of the impossibility of perfect love, but it depends on our continued striving for the love ideal. In Niebuhr's words, justice "is something less than love. Yet it cannot exist without love and remain justice."[9]

Niebuhr argues that we arrive at a social ethic by working out of this tension between love and justice. Cahill describes Niebuhr's approach as follows: "Justice needs to be encouraged by love. And mutual love is the highest possibility of history, but that needs to be stimulated by some element of self-sacrificial love." Justice and love, therefore, are symbiotically related: love motivates the pursuit of justice, and justice helps remove the obstacles that prevent us from loving one another. But we need the example of a particular kind of love—of a love that gives of itself with no expectation of return—to keep us engaged in the pursuit of justice in a broken world.

Thus, while Niebuhr's social ethics starts from a place of pessimism —of acknowledging that conflict between human beings will probably never disappear—it also supplies a basis for appreciating the gains that we do make. Moral transformation in society is difficult and always incomplete, but it is real. Robin Lovin describes this approach: "For Niebuhr it was always important to say you can't transform society just by trying to love your neighbor, but it's equally a part of that message, though maybe a more subtle part, to say you can't transform your society without an idea of love that ultimately stands in judgment on your achievements of justice." Hauerwas succinctly sums up how Niebuhr relates love and

9. D. B. Robertson, ed., *Love and Justice: Selections from the Shorter Writings of Reinhold Niebuhr* (Philadelphia: Westminster, 1957), 28.

justice: "the ideal of sacrificial love making possible relative justice: that's Reinhold Niebuhr."

Niebuhr moves from a more abstract treatment of love and justice to a comprehensive ethical vision through the biblical concept of the kingdom of God. For Niebuhr, the kingdom of God is the state of perfect harmony among human beings. As such, it is an "impossible possibility": although we will never succeed in building the kingdom in this life, we must strive for it nonetheless because we know that it is real. And in our striving, we manage to catch glimpses of the kingdom in human life, in the form of what Cahill calls "the social presence of grace." A vision of the kingdom is key, if not to achieving, then at least to "approximating the kingdom of God here on earth," as Andrew Finstuen puts it.

It is in striving for the kingdom that Niebuhr most clearly reveals himself to be a child of the Social Gospel. For all his concern with squarely facing the depths of sin, he really did believe that human flourishing was possible. Massa says Niebuhr sought to "create enough space in society where people were free to choose the good and groups of people could band together for social purposes to achieve the good." But to do so, they would have to come to terms with the spiritual aspect of the human experience. And this was true irrespective of what a particular individual happened to believe. As Massa observes, "I think what he wanted to construct was the theological message that had to be read by political advisors and sociologists and public pundits and journalists and all kinds of people that made available to them a kind of discourse that had all been forgotten. That is, the discourse of St. Augustine—of original sin, and fallenness, and grace, and the ability to pick ourselves up with grace and dust ourselves off and get on with the business of effecting social change." Cahill adds, "he's a great example of the fact that Christian ethical claims and strategies and agendas should be and are ultimately rooted in theological claims and expectations." Lovin concludes, "that theological understanding keeps us at the task of creating approximate justice as best we can in the situation where we find ourselves."

Given his belief in "approximate justice" grounded by love, what sort of advocate for the kingdom of God did Niebuhr prove to be? For one thing, he was tireless. Between his teaching, preaching, writing, and activism, he managed to fulfill the demands of several careers at once. People have since marveled at how he managed to do so much. In the words of Cornel West: "Talk about energy, talk about the talent, talk about the genius! It was the discipline. When you look at his reading, his teaching,

his lectures, his writing . . . it was no accident he had a stroke in the early
'50s. How could he get it all in? It was unbelievable. But he did! And he
did it with a smile. He did it with a buoyancy of soul."

Yet Niebuhr's life also reveals the extent to which he remained bound
to the perspectives and prejudices of his time and place. For instance, he
went from being ahead of his time in his analysis and activism on race
issues to urging moderation at key junctures of the civil rights movement.
And for all the resources that his thought has to offer from the perspectives of race and class, it has significant shortcomings on issues of gender.
It is to these lingering questions regarding race and gender that we turn.

Race

The degree and quality of Niebuhr's engagement on race issues varied
significantly over the course of his life. Niebuhr first began to take an
activist stance toward race while serving as chair of Detroit's Interracial
Committee in 1926. It was while working on this committee that Niebuhr
appears to have first grappled with the systemic character of race prejudice. Healan Gaston observes that, prior to his time on the committee,
Niebuhr was "most concerned about labor relations and class questions.
Race [was] . . . a somewhat secondary concern." But as he worked with
the committee to address housing issues and the plight of black workers,
he began to develop an awareness of how deeply woven into the social
fabric of Detroit race prejudice was. As chapter 1 illustrates, his efforts
earned him the respect of Detroit's black community. Flawed as his perspective might have been, Niebuhr was one of the few white ministers
willing to invest time and effort in issues of race.

In the early 1930s Niebuhr engaged in some of his sharpest thinking
about race, and his most effective activism. At Union Seminary, Niebuhr
team-taught a course incorporating the work of prominent black intellectuals such as James Weldon Johnson and W. E. B. Du Bois.[10] In 1931
he completed an American Missionary Society–sponsored lecture tour
at black colleges and schools throughout the South. That same year he
helped Myles Horton, one of his students, to create the charter for the
Highlander Folk School, originally designed to help organize labor movements in the Appalachian region (Niebuhr also served on the board of

---

10. Marsh, *Strange Glory*, 106.

directors). The Highlander School become a hub for civil rights activism, providing training in techniques of nonviolent resistance and civil disobedience. Martin Luther King had ties to the Highlander School, and Rosa Parks attended it prior to the Montgomery Bus Boycott. In the mid-1930s Niebuhr was also instrumental in starting the Delta Farm Cooperative, an integrated farming community in Mississippi. Niebuhr was thus connected to some of the influential civil rights projects of the 1930s.

It is no coincidence that Niebuhr produced his most incisive thinking on race in the era that he was most immersed in activism. Consider, for instance, his observation regarding the relationship between racial justice and coercion in *Moral Man and Immoral Society* (1932): "However large the number of individual white men who do and who will identify themselves completely with the Negro cause, the white race will not admit the Negro to equal rights if it is not forced to do so."[11] These are the words of someone who is not merely theorizing about race, but has firsthand experience attempting to agitate for racial justice. He would make similarly pointed observations on race in his subsequent book, *Reflections on the End of an Era* (1934): "If . . . the white man were to expiate his sins committed against the darker races, few white men would have the right to live. They live, partly because they are strong enough to maintain themselves against their enemies and partly because their enemies have not taken vengeance upon them. They survive, in other words, both by the law of nature and by the law of grace."[12]

With the onset of World War II, Niebuhr's attention shifted from domestic to international politics. Still, he accepted a place on the NAACP Legal Defense Fund's "Committee of One Hundred" in 1943—a fact duly noted in Niebuhr's FBI file.[13] In 1944 Niebuhr's *The Children of Light and the Children of Darkness* outlined his distinctive, theologically informed approach to democratic theory. His vision of democracy was rooted in the notion that checks and balances provided the best mechanism for individuals and groups to negotiate social power. By the early 1950s he expressed amazement at the strength of organized labor in the United States and at the growth of the middle class. Neither develop-

11. Sifton, *Reinhold Niebuhr: Major Works*, 333.

12. Reinhold Niebuhr, *Reflections on the End of an Era* (New York: Scribner, 1934), 285-86.

13. Richard Wightman Fox, *Reinhold Niebuhr: A Biography* (Ithaca, NY: Cornell University Press, 1996), 282.

ment would have seemed remotely possible to the Niebuhr who wrote *Moral Man.*

The apparent success of the gradualist checks-and-balances approach shaped Niebuhr's perception of the civil rights movement as it garnered national attention in the 1950s. In 1957, when white violence against blacks broke out in the South in the wake of school integration, Martin Luther King approached Niebuhr about adding his name to a petition asking for President Eisenhower to intervene. Biographer Richard Fox notes that Niebuhr refused on the grounds that it would "do more harm than good" to pressure Eisenhower in such a public way. It was better to arrange a meeting with him in private.[14]

This response has since puzzled Niebuhr's admirers as well as his critics, especially given the role of his early writings in helping to shape the civil rights movement. In his 1963 "Letter from Birmingham Jail," Martin Luther King referenced Niebuhr and his observations about the immorality of group behavior. Civil rights activist Andrew Young, who would go on to serve as a congressman and as mayor of Atlanta, recalls quoting Niebuhr in an argument with King in the mid-1960s. King responded, "you should be ashamed to quote Reinhold Niebuhr that way!" —and proceeded to lecture Young on what Niebuhr had actually said.[15] Young adds, "when I got home I got my *Nature and Destiny of Man* down off the shelf and it was almost as if he were quoting a paragraph verbatim. . . . I am sure he had not touched his copy since the 1950s." Niebuhr's writing was "that powerful . . . that much of an influence." Young continues, "Niebuhr kept us from being naïve . . . about the evil structures of society." He also helped spur the movement's leaders on: "It was almost as if Reinhold Niebuhr was telling us—either you make non-violence work or violence is inevitable. . . . It put a sense of urgency in what we did."

Why did the firebrand of the 1930s grow reticent on these matters in the 1950s? It certainly wasn't for lack of courage. Even late in life, Niebuhr was not one to evade controversy. According to Ursula, Niebuhr was "rather pleased" with a torrent of hate mail he received following the publication of "The King's Chapel and the King's Court" in 1969.[16] Cornel West attributes Niebuhr's hesitancy to the changes in Niebuhr's

---

14. Fox, *Reinhold Niebuhr: A Biography*, 282.

15. Journey Films interview with Andrew Young, May 6, 2016. Unless otherwise noted, subsequent quotes attributed to Young are from this interview.

16. Fox, *Reinhold Niebuhr: A Biography*, 289.

social location. In 1932 he was a "revolutionary Christian and a democratic socialist"; by the late 1940s he had become a "mainstream Cold War liberal." From his establishment perch, Niebuhr had grown leery of the destabilizing effects of sudden social change. West maintains that Niebuhr "was always an anti-racist, and that's very important," but he argues that we still "need to acknowledge the shift that takes place." Hauerwas adds, "I think that he became, in some ways, an establishment figure that would find it very hard to take too radical a position."

Also, Niebuhr's sphere of interaction was much smaller in the mid-1950s. Following his stroke in 1952, he had to essentially give up the activism that had been such a major part of his identity. From the confines of Riverside Drive, he could no longer observe the workings of American society in quite the same way. He thus lacked the breadth of exposure that had fueled his sharpest work. Lovin observes, "At a time when the Civil Rights Movement is gaining ground in the churches and a lot of things are happening in church basements . . . Reinhold Niebuhr is not able to be in those church basements. I think for that reason, he didn't see some of the signs of hope that perhaps a Martin Luther King, Jr. might have seen or for that matter an Abraham Joshua Heschel might have seen. It doesn't mean he wasn't supportive; he was just a little more cautious about the risks that were involved with pushing for equality and a little less aware." Richard Fox observes that Niebuhr's commentaries on race regain something of their former bite in the 1960s. As evidence he cites an article from 1964. "We are in for . . . decades of social revolution," Niebuhr intoned, because of the "despair and hopelessness of young northern blacks. The reason for the despair is obvious, but I for one was slow to gauge its import." It was persistent unemployment, not exclusion from voting booths or public accommodations.[17] This sounds a good deal more like the Niebuhr of the 1930s than the Niebuhr of the 1950s. Niebuhr was once again anticipating sudden and wholesale social change, which diverged from the gradualism he had advocated in the wake of World War II.

Part of Niebuhr's turn may have been the product of his friendship with Heschel. As a participant in civil rights activities, Heschel was in the aforementioned church basements. When Heschel would come back to New York after these stints, it's quite easy to imagine Niebuhr peppering him with questions on their Riverside Drive walks. Perhaps his

17. Fox, *Reinhold Niebuhr: A Biography*, 282.

renewed sharpness on such issues was the product of his relationship with another of the day's great voices of conscience. As Andrew Young recalls, "When Rabbi Heschel showed up it was like the Old Testament prophet . . . coming to Selma." And Niebuhr would have joined in had his health permitted. In a telegram to Martin Luther King, he wrote, "Thank you for your invitation [to join the 1965 civil rights march from Selma to Montgomery]. Only a severe stroke prevents me from accepting it. I hope there will be a massive demonstration of all the citizens with conscience in favor of the elemental human rights of voting and freedom of assembly in your march on Alabama's capital."[18] Even in his state of impaired health, Niebuhr's words still rang with vitality.

Niebuhr was a keen observer of the human scene, and relied heavily on direct contact with people and movements to form his ethical judgments. It took working closely with leaders of the black community in Detroit, lecturing in Negro schools, and helping to launch integrated communities and labor training centers to generate his incisive commentary of the 1930s. When he lost those direct contacts, whether because of running in "establishment" circles or because of his declining health, his perspective could lose its edge. But when other keen observers served as his eyes and ears, he recovered his distinctive voice.

Conceptual aspects of his approach also limited what he perceived. As Gary Dorrien observes, Niebuhr talked about racism as "personal bias," as "egotism of a particular kind writ large." While this was useful for understanding how racism can shape group dynamics, it limited one's ability to analyze the particular forms that racism may take. Dorrien continues, "For all of his passionate argument about the evil of racism, Niebuhr himself doesn't think of racism in . . . structural terms, cultural terms. He doesn't think about white supremacy itself as a structure of power that is based on privilege, that presumes to define what's normal." For example: Niebuhr's work on democratic theory gave him the conceptual framework to speak of racism as a manifestation of group egoism that needed to be mitigated through a social system of checks and balances. But he lacked the language to describe how the system of checks and balances could be rigged to marginalize certain groups while maintaining the illusion of proper function. We cannot address these structural dimensions of racism by calibrating the existing system of checks and balances. Instead, we must fundamentally restructure the way the system operates.

18. Sifton, *Reinhold Niebuhr: Major Works*, 688.

The intellectual transition from racism as egoism writ large to racism as a structural problem required a tremendous imaginative leap, similar in scope to the leap he took to expose the pervasive character of coercion in human life in *Moral Man and Immoral Society*. Following his stroke, he lacked the energy for that kind of foundational intellectual work. Nonetheless, Niebuhr's body of work had enough substance behind it to inspire pivotal figures in the civil rights movement. Noting the "immense passion that he has invested in this subject," Dorrien adds, "just the fact that he is the white American theologian that cares about this, really more than any of his peers, it's easy to miss. And many people have."

Gender

Since the 1960s Niebuhr's work has been subject to considerable criticism from a feminist perspective. The issue boils down to Niebuhr's view of sin—and more specifically, his understanding of pride as the most basic way that sin manifests in human life. This view underlies Niebuhr's contention that human beings are fundamentally egocentric, and that restraining the ego is essential to moral growth. It is also implied in the fact that he makes self-sacrificial love the ideal for which we must strive in our quest for justice.

But is pride as universal as Niebuhr makes it out to be, or is his view of the dynamics of sin and grace limited by his gendered lens? As many feminist scholars point out, pride is more accessible for those who have power, and women have historically been excluded from formal structures of power. As Healan Gaston observes, "Niebuhr's emphasis on sinfulness and on the sin of pride in particular is really troubling to feminists, because it raises questions about who his intended audience is. [It] is a wonderful corrective for the powerful, but what about for the powerless? What about for people who have trouble even taking a strong stand or are hiding their gifts instead of trying to exercise them?" Whereas self-sacrificial love can be difficult to cultivate for those who are in power, the powerless—including but not limited to women—are often conditioned to sacrifice constantly, to downplay their own needs in favor of those of others. They are tempted less by pride than by the "sin of hiding," as feminist theologian Susan Nelson Dunfee puts it. Lisa Cahill elaborates: "For many women the sin, the basic and underlying sin is not pride. It is . . . the running away from, or hiding from, the challenge to have an identity and to really make a difference and to have commitments and plans and principles that one courageously pursues and defends, no matter what the obstacles." As Cahill argues, an understanding of sin and grace that speaks to these sorts of spiritual struggles requires different points of emphasis: "What women need is not to be told that they are excessively proud, the remedy for which is love and self-sacrifice . . . rather they need to be told not to completely dissipate their own agency . . . through acts of self-sacrifice to other people."

Our understandings of sin and grace, therefore, must take into account where the individual's moral journey starts. For feminists, too little ego can be as big a moral problem as too much ego. As Cornel West observes, "it's not a question of too much ego sometimes, it's a question of thinking one is worthy to be involved in the quest for self-determination." For those who struggle with this sense of unworthiness, grace calls them to build up rather than break down their sense of self.

The feminist critique has raised the question: Who else in society struggles with a lack of a sense of self? They tend to be people who find themselves on the margins of society, be it on account of gender, race, sexual orientation, or any number of other reasons. Gaston observes that Niebuhr's theology "speaks to the predicament of the powerful." It applies most directly to those who have the ego strength to obtain and wield power. Yet it also offers an arresting vision of how power operates in society. Gaston continues, "Niebuhr gives the oppressed a very compelling line about power in the world. One that might have profound implications for how the individual self would then move forward." It may not always help the powerless in their quest for self-determination; but it does help them understand the power dynamics around them. And this, too, is key to overcoming the "sin of hiding."

The feminist critique is a valuable corrective, not simply to Niebuhr, but to Christian thought more generally. The tendency to view pride as the paradigmatic form of sin runs deep in Christianity, and no doubt reflects the fact that the Christian intellectual tradition has been shaped overwhelmingly by men who held considerable power. Niebuhr devoted his efforts toward enacting justice in the context of a society shaped by the egotism of groups. Those who manage to exert a shaping influence on society rarely lack for ego strength. One wonders if Niebuhr might have formulated his understanding of sin and grace a bit differently had he not been so relentlessly focused on the sociopolitical arena.

These critiques of Niebuhr from the perspectives of race and gender challenge us to revisit different aspects of his ethics. The race-based critiques suggest the need to refine Niebuhr's understanding of justice. More particularly, they push us to reconsider how we think about and address *structural* injustice. The gender-based critiques point to the need for a more refined vision of love: Should we only strive for the ideal of self-sacrificial love? Or might we need to learn to love ourselves as well as our neighbors? But neither critique undermines the underlying logic of Niebuhr's ethic: that to achieve justice, we need to strive for an ideal of love; that to achieve human flourishing, we must strive for the kingdom of God.

Religion

Niebuhr spent his career trying to get people in church pews to think about how they engaged the broader world. He also made the case to nonreligious people that all human beings acted on religious impulses. In Niebuhr's view, we all worship something. A simple way to figure out what we worship is to ask: Where do we find our sense of meaning? That which gives our lives deeper meaning is that which we worship. If we do not worship God—if we do not seek and find our purpose in relationship with our Creator—we seek meaning in an endless array of other things. Political causes, charismatic people, or even one's own ego could become an object of worship.

Because of this impulse to worship, Niebuhr believed, human collectives routinely take on cult-like characteristics. Niebuhr often accused Nazism and communism of functioning as "secular religions," complete with their own deities, rituals, and priests. As the world wars and the rise of the Cold War made painfully clear, nations can incite and channel patriotic fervor into cultish devotion to country. Even the trivial or abstract could take on cult-like characteristics: Niebuhr himself referenced the cult of the automobile, the cult of the proletariat, and the cult of Henry Ford. Wherever the social impulse meets the urge to worship, a cult can form.

For Niebuhr, then, the human experience was shot through with religious characteristics. There was no way to cordon off religion from the rest of life. That is why, in the Cold War era, Niebuhr was put off by attempts to distinguish between the "godly" West and "godless" communism: no human being, much less a whole society, is truly godless.

The distinction that mattered for him was between true religion and false religion. And the litmus test distinguishing the two was simple. As Niebuhr put it in his 1958 interview with Mike Wallace: "My personal attitude toward atheists is the same attitude that I have toward Christians, and would be governed by a very orthodox text: 'By their fruits shall ye know them.'"

Unsurprisingly, Niebuhr gauged these fruits using the weights and measures of ethics. For Niebuhr, we are all caught up in the same drama of sin and redemption. And when the drama concludes we will be judged by our deeds, which will reveal what we worshiped.

Because he was attuned to how religious patterns of behavior seep into everyday life, he was especially good at illuminating the religious character of the American experiment. The fact that America is a secular nation did not preclude it from having a deeply religious sense of itself. Mark Massa explains, "People who say, 'Religious impulses have no bearing on American public life,' don't know what they're talking about. Because from the very beginning, religious impulses and political impulses have been twined together so carefully that it's impossible to take them apart. What we separated were the institutions of church and state, not the impulses of religion and politics."

The key question, then, is not *whether* religion and politics are connected, but *how*. And Niebuhr offered a compelling read of the particular ways in which these impulses combine and manifest in a pluralistic, democratic American context. In Massa's view, Niebuhr "fulfilled the absolutely essential role of a public theologian in the twentieth century: someone who explains the meaning of America in traditional and sometimes not so traditional religious terms."

While Niebuhr understood America to be a religious nation, he did not see it as a Christian nation. For Niebuhr, the very attempt to apply the label of "Christian" to a political system misunderstood the political role of Christianity. As Robin Lovin notes, "One of the things that Niebuhr says is look; we need to understand that there is no Christian system of politics or economics. It's not a matter of choosing one or the other and then deciding it's the Christian system. The Christian attitude towards every system of politics and economics is to ask what kind of justice is it going to produce in this immediate situation and to be prepared to choose the solution that offers us the best approximation of justice." Niebuhr applied a similar litmus test to political and economic systems as he did to individuals: "by your fruits ye shall know them." People of faith should always try to nudge the particular social order in which they find themselves toward greater justice. And they must be willing to resist attempts to obscure injustice through appeals to religious sentiment.

Niebuhr's critiques of religion and politics in America were rooted in a deep love of God and country. Dorrien observes, "Reinhold Niebuhr's someone on his knees at night praying. And for whom giving testimony, being a witness to the saving acts of God in history defines his work." Niebuhr expressed this love by refusing to allow religious pretentiousness or moral complacency to go unnoticed. Niebuhr is often criticized for not articulating an account of what makes Christian faith community distinct from other forms of community. If deeds are what ultimately matter, how do Christian practices such as prayer, confession, and communion help Christian communities become better advocates for justice? Niebuhr wrote comparatively little on such matters, in part because he took a vibrant American church culture for granted. Hauerwas notes, "Theologians oftentimes do not give an account of that which they can presume, and he presumed the vitality of mainstream Protestantism. He himself could count on the church just being there." In this environment, he positioned himself as someone who relentlessly spurred communities of faith to action. But as Hauerwas points out, "we can't count on the church just being there any longer." The 1950s saw the largest growth in church membership that the United States had ever seen. All but a select few Christian denominations have been shrinking in membership ever since. It is no longer possible to assume the kind of broad cultural knowledge of Christian ritual and community that pertained in Niebuhr's era.

Despite his lack of explication on church rituals and traditions, Niebuhr did leave us with a compelling image of the church. Andrew Finstuen quotes a 1955 interview in which Niebuhr compared it to Noah's ark: "Despite the storm without and the smell within, [the church] points to a truth beyond its own stating of it."[19] For all their dysfunction ("the smell within"), churches are a spiritual refuge amid the tumult of a broken world. In this refuge, we learn to be receptive to the grace that both heals us and strengthens us; but once we've been strengthened, we must go back into the fray.

---

19. Andrew Finstuen, *Original Sin and Everyday Protestants* (Chapel Hill: University of North Carolina Press, 2009), 113.

The Voice of Conscience

Niebuhr's life and work defy easy categorization. Over the course of his career, he took on multiple roles: pastor, preacher, professor, social activist, journalist, cultural critic, political theorist—the list goes on. Although he managed to excel at virtually everything he did, he never entirely fit in. Healan Gaston observes, "At every step of Reinhold Niebuhr's career he walked into spaces and was the sort of country bumpkin of the group. [But] it was only a matter of time before he won the respect of each group that he encountered . . . as he made his way into a position of tremendous authority in American culture." She continues, "Niebuhr had a sort of searching quality, a restlessness about him that couldn't be contained." Cornel West notes, "Reinhold Niebuhr was like a jazz man. He had his own voice. It was distinctive, it was dissonant."

It was precisely this dissonant quality that gave Niebuhr's voice its conscience-rousing edge. He was perpetually aware of how every audience he spoke to and every group he was a part of fell short of the ethical ideal. Even when he became preeminent within a given group, he retained the ability to see that group from an outsider's vantage point. David Brooks explains the importance of this trait: "Richard Rohr, a Catholic theologian, has a concept 'on the inside of the edge.' And that means, when you're inside your group, it's surrounded by a boundary. And where you want to be is not in the middle of your group, but just inside the edge of your group. And that way you can see the problems with your group, and you can be a link to people outside your group, and you can practice proper self-criticism. And Niebuhr was very good at that, proper self-criticism."

Persistently positioning oneself as a voice of conscience requires courage in various forms. One form is the courage to make sweeping claims that have high moral stakes. Brooks observes that, on an intellectual level, people like Niebuhr and Heschel were "going for the big bite. They were going to influence the whole culture and not just people within their own [religion]." Making such broad arguments can leave one vulnerable to criticism: "[Niebuhr] is taking big risks in his books. When you write on big subjects, you're just laying yourself open to super-criticism." A case in point is *Moral Man and Immoral Society*, which was subjected to vicious critique following its publication. Today, it is considered one of the most influential religious texts of the twentieth century.

Additionally, being a voice of conscience requires the courage to change one's mind. Societies are in a state of constant change, and each change brings new ethical challenges and possibilities. Voices of conscience must be willing to take these changes into account—and sometimes, this requires altering one's public stance on a given issue. This is bound to upset people, as Brooks observes: "When you change your mind in public and if you're a public figure and public intellectual, your friends hate you and your enemies hate you more. You would think if you said, 'I was wrong, I actually agree with these people,' [former opponents] would welcome you with open arms. But that's not the way the world works. They sense weakness in you and they pounce. And so when someone would break ranks or change sides, often you're alienating everyone all at once."

Niebuhr significantly altered his position on a variety of issues, from pacifism, to Marxism, to how to deal with the Soviet Union. As Gary Dorrien notes, "Niebuhr basically changed his politics every ten years." With each change, there was a group of people who thought he had sold out. Many Social Gospelers certainly thought so after the publication of *Moral Man*. So did his pacifist colleagues when he published "An End to Illusions" on the eve of World War II.

Whenever public figures change their mind, they leave themselves vulnerable to the criticism that they have compromised their principles. Sometimes the criticism is valid. But other times, moral integrity requires the courage to change. For instance: when pacifist German theologian Dietrich Bonhoeffer was confronted with the ghastly realities of the Nazi regime, he chose to participate in a plot to assassinate Hitler. While many pacifists disagreed with this decision, few questioned his moral integrity. Bonhoeffer admittedly faced an extraordinary predicament. But his example demonstrates that moral integrity requires the willingness to change one's mind as well as the willingness to be steadfast.

Did Niebuhr change his mind in ways that compromised his integrity? Our contributors do not think so. Cahill notes, "I would not say that there was a real change in his basic convictions. But the emphasis and what he felt really needed to be lifted up did change." For all the ways that he disagrees with Niebuhr, Hauerwas maintains, "he made his way among very powerful people, both intellectually and politically, with great integrity. And I admire that." West observes, "part of the greatness of Reinhold Niebuhr, is that he was willing to risk unpopularity in the name of integrity." Niebuhr both took controversial stands and revisited his positions in ways that enabled him to retain a prophetic edge.

Voices of conscience must also have an audience. This brings us to the final trait that enabled Niebuhr to inhabit this role: namely, his ability to speak to the concerns of a broad cross section of American society. From the nation's inception, American society has been dazzlingly diverse. As Andrew Burnaby observed in 1760, "fire and water are not more heterogeneous than the different colonies of North America." Over the course of our history, the challenge confronting every prominent public figure has been how to craft a message that resonates with the dizzying variety of groups that make up a democratic pluralist society. Few in American history have succeeded as Niebuhr has at addressing such complex issues in such a broadly accessible way.

Mark Massa uses the Latin term *pontifex* to describe Niebuhr. We typically associate the term with the pope, who is referred to as *pontifex maximus* (this is also where we derive the English term "pontiff"). But Massa points out that, in Latin, *pontifex* means "bridge builder": "I think Reinhold Niebuhr is a *pontifex*. He's a bridge builder between the inside of the Christian tradition which has become overly concerned with itself . . . and the concerns of the vast majority of people, whether they're religious or not. But they have a deep need to understand themselves as a part of some larger purpose, some larger meaning." Niebuhr was able to draw on the rich history of Christian thought—a history steeped in concepts such as sin and grace, judgment and mercy, and love and justice—to build bridges between various groups in society that, for all their differences, shared a common set of hopes and fears. Massa continues, "Reinhold Niebuhr recognized that after Nagasaki and Hiroshima, the world indeed was a scary and dangerous place. And he believed that the religious tradition of the West had something important and meaningful to say to where America found itself after 1945 as the country that had dropped the atomic bombs. . . . He believed that there was something there that was compelling and true that had to be told, and a lot of people listened to him telling those stories." Niebuhr's ability to critique his own communities gave his words their prophetic power; but it was his knack for building bridges that made him a voice of conscience.

The Edge of the Abyss: Reinhold Niebuhr Today

In what ways might Niebuhr's mid-twentieth-century voice speak to our own time and place? After all, the immediate concerns that occupied

Niebuhr at midcentury are quite different from our own. Robin Lovin observes, "Reinhold Niebuhr is the kind of thinker whose legacy in one sense is always at risk because so much of what he has said is said to particular issues that he dealt with in his own time and he's apt to seem either out of touch or out of date." Niebuhr's impassioned arguments for intervention in World War II, for instance, might not seem particularly noteworthy in light of the prominent American role in world politics since Pearl Harbor. Yet, however out of sync the particulars of his analysis might seem at times, his underlying worldview—what this study has depicted as a God's-eye view of human affairs—continues to attract those both within and outside the Christian tradition. As David Brooks puts it, "Niebuhr is a sort of gateway drug to religion."

Niebuhr's enduring appeal involved more than just his perspective. He also had a unique way with words. As a student at Union in the 1950s, former congressman and mayor of Indianapolis Bill Hudnut recalls being awestruck by Niebuhr's use of language: "I used to say him and William Faulkner, back in the '50s, were the two people I admired most for their command of English." Niebuhr knew how to catch a reader's attention. Andrew Bacevich observes that Niebuhr "has a real knack for providing the phrase that captures an idea," which can then be "easily extracted . . . to use as a very quotable quote." In a similar vein, Hauerwas quips, "I've learned a hell of a lot from [Niebuhr] in terms of how to write a provocative sentence." This ability has helped Niebuhr gain traction in our sound-bite culture. Elisabeth Sifton notes that, in the age of social media, "everything has to be understood instantly or misunderstood—there's not a possibility of genuine human intercourse in all of that." Yet Niebuhr has still managed to work his way into contemporary conversations. As journalist Paul Elie observed in 2007, "a well-turned Niebuhr reference is the speechwriter's equivalent of a photo op with Bono."[20]

As in his own day, Niebuhr continues to be referenced by voices that span the political spectrum. Brooks lists Niebuhr alongside British author George Orwell as one of the "midcentury figures that everybody wants to claim for their own. . . . These writers transcend modern categories, and they can be used by people of a lot of different persuasions." This sort of broad appeal is remarkably rare in our polarized cultural climate.

20. Paul Elie, "A Man for All Reasons," *Atlantic*, November 2007, http://www.the-atlantic.com/magazine/archive/2007/11/a-man-for-all-reasons/306337/.

As Gaston observes, "there is a Reinhold in there somewhere that can inspire almost anyone."

Part of Niebuhr's enduring appeal stems from the fact that his observations help us understand and critique our contemporary context. Andrew Bacevich cites Niebuhr's observations on American self-conception: "American ambition. The American interpretation of American power. The American conviction that we are in some way the new chosen people. Those warnings are as prescient today as they were when he voiced them." Cornel West thinks of Niebuhr at every State of the Union address: "America has a religion of possibilities, no constraints, no limits we cannot go beyond because we are Americans. We hear it every January, in the president's State of the Union. . . . Niebuhr would disagree with that. He said, 'No, we're human beings who have limits like anybody else.'"

But Niebuhr's actual words are only one facet of his enduring relevance. He also supplies a template for cultivating our own voices of conscience: people who subject contemporary American life to moral scrutiny in terms that resonate with a broad audience. Robin Lovin observes that it is especially challenging to do this given how fragmented our public discourse has become: "we've got innumerable outlets for our writing, but we're never read except by the people who already agree with us." For Lovin, Niebuhr was able to reach a broad cross section of his own culture because he was "creating a moral vocabulary for the public." People who are "doing today what Niebuhr did, are the people who are trying to figure out where do we find that kind of moral vocabulary to make choices today." When asked to define her father's legacy, Elisabeth Sifton responded, "I can't define a Niebuhrian legacy but I know it when I see it. . . . [It] would be a receptivity to understanding the ironic contradictions at the heart of American life and trying make them work for the good."

Niebuhr's legacy certainly lives on in some of our own most incisive voices on matters of faith and politics. In the words of Hauerwas, "I not only admire Niebuhr, I love him. I disagree with almost everything that he said. But . . . that he made possible the importance of disagreeing with him is a great gift." West sums up the sentiments of many who have been inspired by Niebuhr and his legacy: "Reinhold Niebuhr makes me shake and tremble as a human being when I think of the depths of his courage, his vision, his determination, his discipline, his willingness to expose himself publicly, and continually grow and mature . . . that's why I consider him a soul mate. That's why when I think of his name, I think of John Coltrane, or Anton Chekov, or Rabbi Abraham Joshua Heschel. These are the special spirits of the species, who have the courage to go to the edge of life's abyss to step out on nothing and land on something."

Times may change, but the abyss remains with us. May Niebuhr's voice and example grant us the serenity, courage, and wisdom to step out.

Bibliography

Bacevich, Andrew J. Introduction to *The Irony of American History*, by Reinhold Niebuhr. Chicago: University of Chicago Press, 2008.

Barth, Karl. "No Christian Marshall Plan." *Christian Century*, December 8, 1948.

Beinart, Peter. *The Icarus Syndrome: A History of American Hubris*. New York: HarperCollins, 2010.

Cahill, Lisa Sowle. *Global Justice, Christology, and Christian Ethics*. New York: Cambridge University Press, 2013.

Carnahan, Kevin. "Recent Work on Reinhold Niebuhr." *Religion Compass* 5, no. 8 (2011): 365–75.

Chambers, Whittaker. "Faith for a Lenten Age." *Time*, March 8, 1948.

Coffman, Elesha J. *The* Christian Century *and the Rise of the Protestant Mainline*. New York: Oxford University Press, 2013.

Cone, James H. *The Cross and the Lynching Tree*. Maryknoll, NY: Orbis, 2011.

Dorrien, Gary J. "Christian Realism: Reinhold Niebuhr's Theology, Ethics, and Politics." In *Reinhold Niebuhr: Engagements with an American Original*, edited by Daniel Rice, 22–38. Grand Rapids: Eerdmans, 2009.

Elie, Paul. "A Man for All Reasons." *Atlantic*, November 2007.

Feldman, Egal. "Reinhold Niebuhr and the Jews." *Jewish Social Studies* 46 (March 4, 1984).

Finstuen, Andrew. *Original Sin and Everyday Protestants*. Chapel Hill: University of North Carolina Press, 2009.

———. "The Prophet and the Evangelist." *Books and Culture*, July/August 2006.

Fox, Richard Wightman. *Reinhold Niebuhr: A Biography*. Ithaca, NY: Cornell University Press, 1996.

Gaston, K. Healan. "'A Bad Kind of Magic': The Niebuhr Brothers on 'Utilitarian Christianity' and the Defense of Democracy." *Harvard Theological Review*, no. 107 (January 2014).

Gilkey, Langdon. *On Niebuhr*. Chicago: University of Chicago Press, 2001.

Halliwell, Martin. *The Constant Dialogue: Reinhold Niebuhr and American Intellectual Culture*. New York: Rowman and Littlefield, 2005.

Herzog, Jonathan. *The Spiritual-Industrial Complex*. New York: Oxford University Press, 2011.

Inboden, William. "The Prophetic Conflict: Reinhold Niebuhr, Christian Realism, and World War II." *Diplomatic History*, no. 38 (January 2014).

Kegley Charles W., and Robert W. Bretall, eds. *Reinhold Niebuhr: His Religious, Social, and Political Thought*. New York: Macmillan, 1956.

Landon, Harold R., ed. *Reinhold Niebuhr: A Prophetic Voice in Our Time*. Greenwich, CT: Seabury Press, 1962.

Littell, Franklin. "Reinhold Niebuhr and the Jewish People." *Holocaust and Genocide Studies*, no. 6 (January 1991).

Lovin, Robin W. *Christian Realism and the New Realism and the New Realities*. New York: Cambridge University Press, 2008.

———. *Reinhold Niebuhr and Christian Realism*. Cambridge: Cambridge University Press, 1995.

Massa, Mark S. *Catholics and American Culture: Fulton Sheen, Dorothy Day, and the Notre Dame Football Team*. New York: Crossroad, 1999.

Merkley, Paul. *Reinhold Niebuhr: A Political Account*. Montreal: McGill-Queens University Press, 1975.

Meyer, Donald. *The Protestant Search for Political Realism*. Middletown, CT: Wesleyan University Press, 1988.

Miles, Rebekah. "Uncredited: Was Ursula Niebuhr Reinhold's Coathor?" *Christian Century*, January 25, 2012.

Morris, Daniel. "'The Pull of Love': Mutual Love as Democratic Virtue in Niebuhrian Political Theology." *Political Theology* (February 2016).

Niebuhr, Reinhold. "Continental vs. Anglo-Saxon Theology," *Christian Century*, December 8, 1948.

———. "The Death of a Martyr." *Christianity and Crisis* 5, no. 11 (June 25, 1945).

———. "The Failure of German-Americanism." *Atlantic* 118 (July 1916): 13–18.

———. *An Interpretation of Christian Ethics*. Louisville: Westminster John Knox, 2013.

——. "The King's Chapel and the King's Court." *Christianity and Crisis* (August 4, 1969).

——. *Leaves from the Notebook of a Tamed Cynic.* Louisville: Westminster John Knox, 1980.

——. *The Nature and Destiny of Man.* New York: Scribner, 1943.

——. "The Problem of the Hyphen." *Atlantic,* July 1916.

——. *Reflections on the End of an Era.* New York: Scribner, 1934.

——. "Toward New Intra-Christian Endeavors," *Christian Century,* December 31, 1969.

——. "We Are Men and Not God." *Christian Century,* October 27, 1948.

Plaskow, Judith. *Sex, Sin, and Grace: Women's Experience and the Theologies of Reinhold Niebuhr and Paul Tillich.* Washington, DC: University Press of America, 1980.

Quinley, Harold E., and Charles Y. Glock. *Antisemitism in America.* New Brunswick, NJ: Transaction Books, 1983.

Rasmussen, Larry, ed. *Reinhold Niebuhr: Theologian of Public Life.* Minneapolis: Fortress, 1991.

Rice, Daniel F. *Reinhold Niebuhr and His Circle of Influence.* New York: Cambridge University Press, 2013.

——. *Reinhold Niebuhr and John Dewey: An American Odyssey.* Albany: SUNY Press, 1993.

Robertson, D. B., ed. *Love and Justice: Selections from the Shorter Writings of Reinhold Niebuhr.* Philadelphia: Westminster, 1957.

Sabella, Jeremy. "Establishment Radical: Assessing the Legacy of Reinhold Niebuhr's *Reflections on the End of an Era.*" *Political Theology* (June 2016).

Schlesinger, Arthur, Jr. *A Life in the Twentieth Century: Innocent Beginnings, 1917–1950.* New York: Houghton Mifflin, 2000.

——. *The Vital Center: The Politics of Freedom.* New Brunswick, NJ: Transaction Publishers, 1970.

Shapiro, Fred R. "Who Wrote the Serenity Prayer?" *Chronicle of Higher Education,* April 28, 2014.

Sifton, Elisabeth, ed. *Reinhold Niebuhr: Major Works.* New York: Library of America, 2015.

——. *The Serenity Prayer: Faith and Politics in Times of Peace and War.* New York: Norton, 2005.

Silk, Mark. *Spiritual Politics: Religion and America Since World War II.* New York: Simon and Schuster, 1988.

Stone, Ronald. *Professor Reinhold Niebuhr: A Mentor to the Twentieth Century*. Louisville: Westminster John Knox, 1992.

Wacker, Grant. *America's Pastor: Billy Graham and the Shaping of a Nation*. Cambridge, MA: Harvard University Press, Belknap Press, 2014.

West, Cornel. Foreword to *Moral Man and Immoral Society*, by Reinhold Niebuhr. Louisville: Westminster John Knox, 2014.

White, E. B., ed. *The United Nations Fight for the Four Freedoms*. Washington, DC: Government Printing Office, 1942.

A Note on Archival Sources

Interview transcripts are the property of Journey Films, 1413 King St., Alexandria, Virginia.

Niebuhr family correspondence is part of the Reinhold Niebuhr Papers, Library of Congress.

Contributors

ANDREW J. BACEVICH is Professor Emeritus of International Relations and History at Boston University. A graduate of the US Military Academy, he received his PhD in American diplomatic history from Princeton University. Before joining the faculty of Boston University, he taught at West Point and Johns Hopkins. He is the author of *America's War for the Greater Middle East: A Military History* (Random House, 2016).

DAVID BROOKS is an author, cultural critic, and commentator. A *New York Times* columnist, he appears regularly on *PBS NewsHour*, NPR's *All Things Considered*, and NBC's *Meet the Press*. He teaches at Yale University and is the author of the critically acclaimed book, *The Road to Character* (Random House, 2015).

LISA SOWLE CAHILL received her BA from Santa Clara University and her MA and PhD from the University of Chicago Divinity School. She has taught at Boston College since 1976, and has been a visiting professor at Georgetown and Yale Universities. Her research interests include bioethics, ethics of sex and gender, social ethics, and Catholic social teaching. She is the author of *Global Justice, Christology, and Christian Ethics* (Cambridge University Press, 2013).

JIMMY CARTER is the thirty-ninth president of the United States and founder of the Carter Center. He was a naval submarine officer from 1946 to 1952 before serving as governor of Georgia (1971–1975) and as president (1977–1981). Following his presidency, Carter has established himself as one of the world's premier humanitarians. He was awarded the Nobel Peace Prize in 2002.

GARY DORRIEN is the Reinhold Niebuhr Professor of Social Ethics at Union Theological Seminary and Professor of Religion at Columbia University. An Episcopal priest, he was previously the Parfet Distinguished Professor at Kalamazoo College. His book *Kantian Reason and Hegelian Spirit: The Idealistic Logic of Modern Theology* (Wiley Blackwell, 2012) won the Association of American Publishers' PROSE Award in 2013.

ANDREW FINSTUEN is the Dean of the Honors College at Boise State, Associate Professor in the Department of History, and producer of the *American Conscience* documentary. He codirected the "Worlds of Billy Graham" project and is the author of the award-winning book *Original Sin and Everyday Protestants* (University of North Carolina Press, 2009).

K. HEALAN GASTON is a lecturer on American religious history at Harvard Divinity School and consultant for the *American Conscience* project. As president of the Niebuhr Society, she coordinated the film's November 2016 debut at the American Academy of Religion conference. She is the author of "'A Bad Kind of Magic': The Niebuhr Brothers on 'Utilitarian Christianity' and the Defense of Democracy," *Harvard Theological Review* 107, no. 1 (January 2014) and is currently writing a book on the "prophetic pluralism" of the Niebuhr brothers.

STANLEY HAUERWAS is the Gilbert T. Rowe Professor Emeritus of Divinity and Law at Duke Divinity School. Widely recognized as one of the most influential thinkers in theological ethics, Hauerwas delivered the Gifford Lectures in 2000 and was named "America's Best Theologian" by *Time* magazine in 2001. Hauerwas is the author of *With the Grain of the Universe: The Church's Witness and Natural Theology* (Brazos Press, 2001).

SUSANNAH HESCHEL is the Eli Black Professor and Chair of the Jewish Studies Program at Dartmouth College. Her scholarship focuses on Jewish and Christian components in German thought during the nineteenth and twentieth centuries, and she is the author of *Abraham Geiger and the Jewish Jesus* (University of Chicago Press, 1998) and *The Aryan Jesus: Christian Theologians and the Bible in Nazi Germany* (Princeton University Press, 2010). The recipient of research grants from the Carnegie, Ford, and Rockefeller Foundations, she is currently a Guggenheim Fellow and writing a book on the history of European Jewish scholarship on Islam.

WILLIAM H. HUDNUT III (1932–2016) was a former congressman and mayor of Indianapolis. Upon obtaining a Masters of Divinity degree from Union Theological Seminary in 1957, he was ordained a minister in the Presbyterian Church. After serving a term in the US Congress from 1973 to 1975, Hudnut was elected mayor of Indianapolis, a post he held for sixteen years. He is the author of *Changing Metropolitan America: Planning for a More Sustainable Future* (2008).

ROBIN W. LOVIN is the William H. Scheide Senior Fellow at the Center of Theological Inquiry (CTI) in Princeton, New Jersey, and Cary Maguire University Professor of Ethics Emeritus at Southern Methodist University. A resident scholar at CTI since 2012, he became a member of the SMU faculty in 1994, and served as Dean of SMU's Perkins School of Theology from 1994 to 2002. An expert on Niebuhr's life and thought, Dr. Lovin is the author of *Reinhold Niebuhr and Christian Realism* (Cambridge University Press, 1995) and *Christian Realism and the New Realities* (Cambridge University Press, 2008).

FR. MARK S. MASSA, SJ, was educated at the University of Detroit, the University of Chicago, and Harvard University. Fr. Massa has taught at Fordham University, served as Dean of Boston College's School of Theology and Ministry, and currently directs the Boisi Center for Religion and Public Life at Boston College. His award-winning book *Catholics and American Culture* (Crossroad, 2005) used Niebuhr's concept of irony as a lens through which to examine twentieth-century American Catholicism.

ELISABETH SIFTON is a writer and retired book publisher. The daughter of Reinhold and Ursula Niebuhr, she is the author of *The Serenity Prayer: Faith and Politics in Times of Peace and War* (Norton, 2003); coauthor with her late husband, Fritz Stern, of *No Ordinary Men: Dietrich Bonhoeffer and Hans von Dohnanyi; Resisters against Hitler in Church and State* (New York Review Books, 2013); and editor of the Library of America's *Reinhold Niebuhr: Major Works on Religion and Politics* (Library of America, 2015).

RONALD H. STONE is the John Witherspoon Professor Emeritus of Christian Ethics at Pittsburgh Theological Seminary. During his studies at Union Theological Seminary, Dr. Stone had the distinction of serving as Reinhold Niebuhr's final graduate assistant. He is the author of *Faith and Politics: Reinhold Niebuhr and Paul Tillich at Union Seminary in New York* (Mercer University Press, 2012).

CORNEL WEST is Professor of Philosophy and Christian Practice at Union Theological Seminary and Professor Emeritus at Princeton University. He has also taught at Yale, Harvard, and the University of Paris. In addition to his acclaimed scholarship, Dr. West is a tireless activist who has contributed to numerous social movements, documentaries, and spoken word albums. He is the author of *Race Matters* (Beacon Press, 2001).

ANDREW YOUNG is a former congressman, mayor of Atlanta, and Presidential Medal of Freedom recipient. After graduating from Howard University and Hartford Theological Seminary, Young worked alongside Martin Luther King in the civil rights movement and helped draft both the Civil Rights Act and the Voting Rights Act. He is the author of *An Easy Burden: The Civil Rights Movement and the Transformation of America* (HarperCollins, 1996).

Index